New Orleans, Louisiana

COPYRIGHT ©2016 by Dr. Scharmaine L. Baker and its licensors.
All rights reserved.

No part of this book may be reproduced or transmitted in any form or by any means, electronic or mechanical, including photocopy, recording, or by any information storage and retrieval system without the written permission of the publisher or author except where permitted by law.

For information address A DrNurse Publishing House
2475 Canal Street, Suite 105, New Orleans, La. 70119
www.NolatheNurse.com

ISBN-13: 978-1-945088-06-3
ISBN-10: 1-945088-06-3

Author Contact info:
DrBakerNP@NolaTheNurse.com

www.DrBakerNP.com
www.NolaTheNurse.com

Nola the Nurse®

Activity Book for Kindergarten

Volume 2

by Dr. Scharmaine L. Baker NP

Illustrated by Marvin Alonso

Match the same pictures.

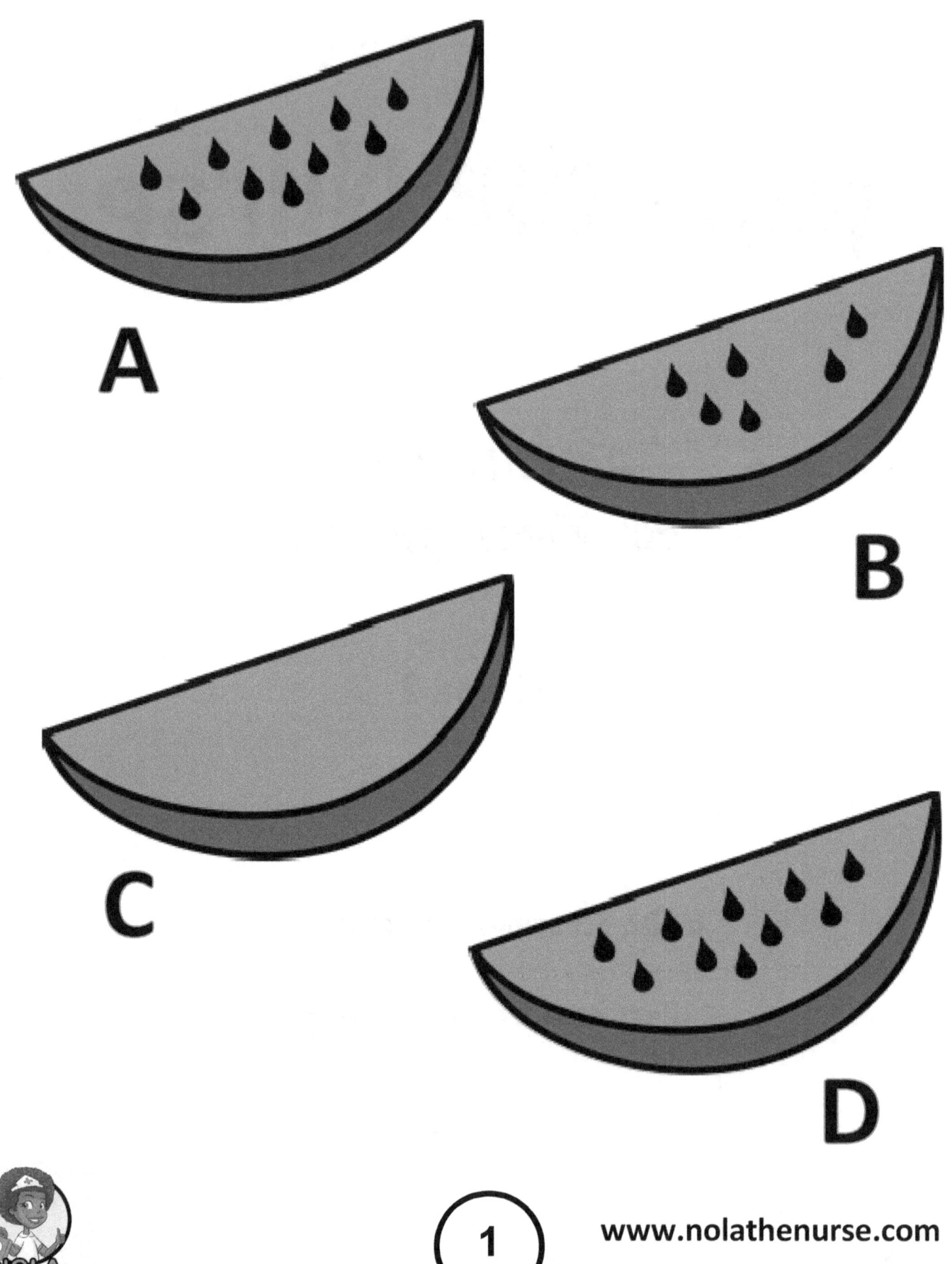

Check [✓] the missing part of the picture.

Help the Panda to find her baby panda.

Find five differences between these two images.

Rearrange the jumbled pieces of the given picture.

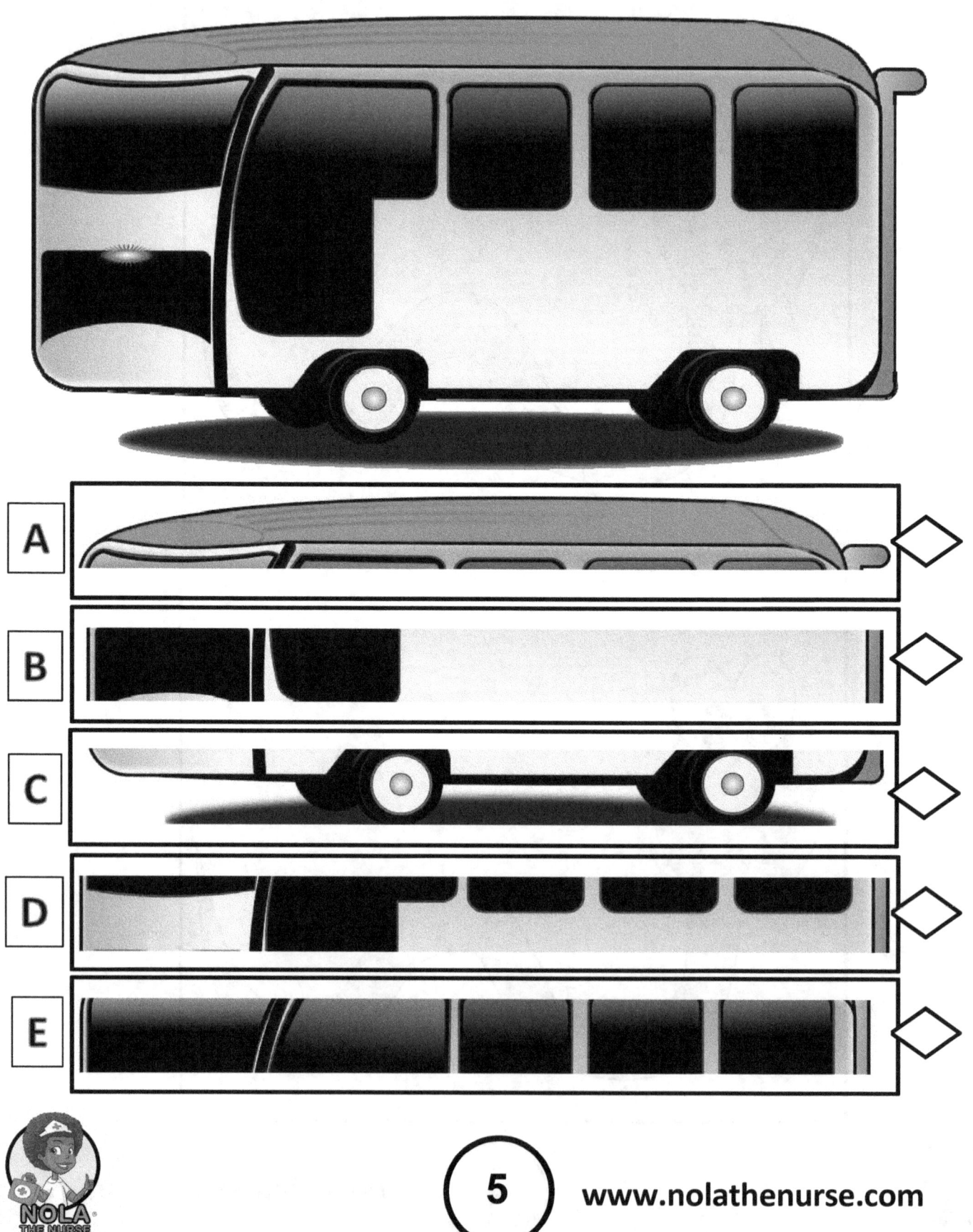

Draw the missing picture in the given space.

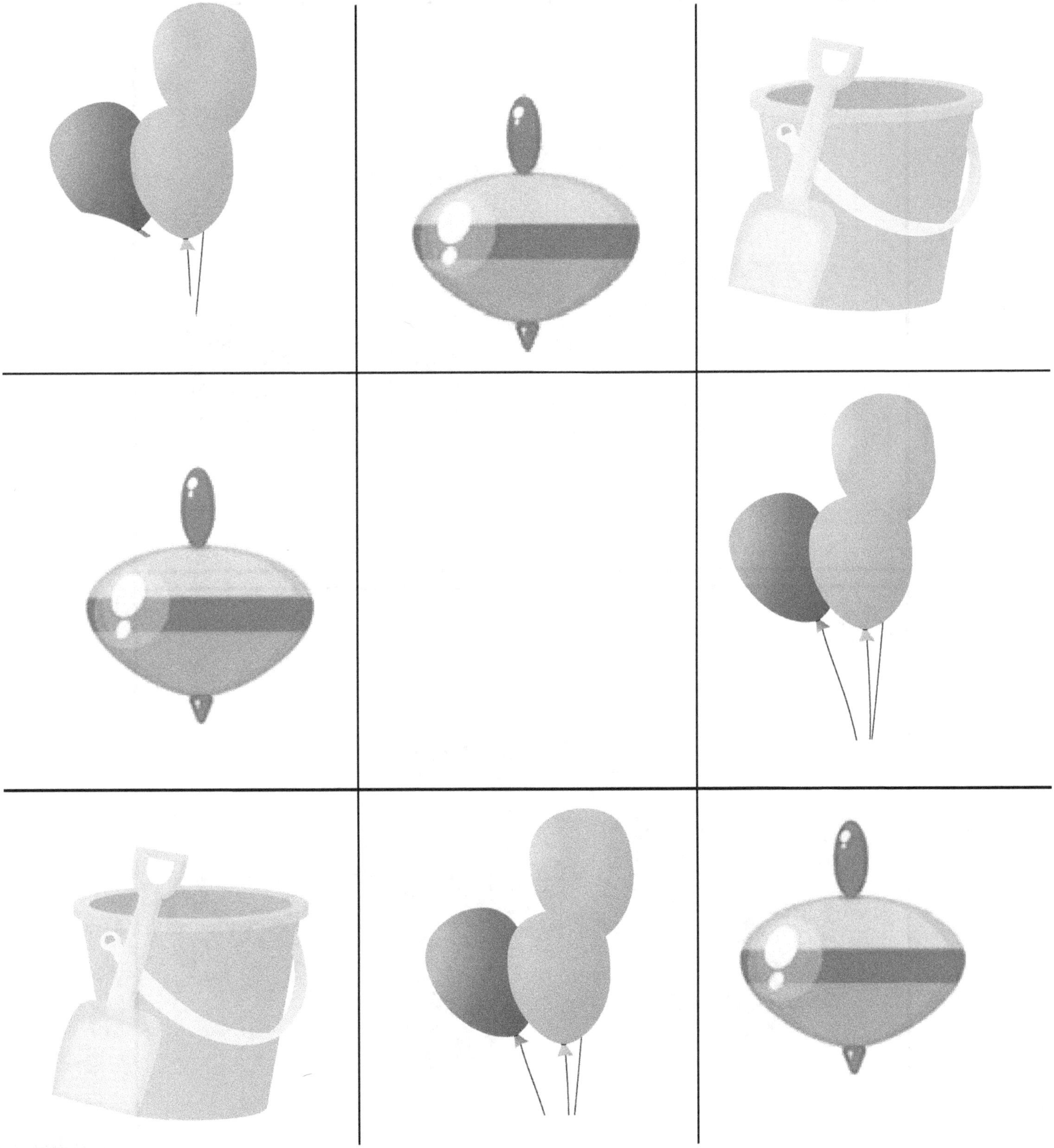

6

Spot five differences between these two pictures.

Look at the filled boxes carefully and complete the patterns in the blank boxes.

Charo The CRNA

Check [✓] the two identical pictures.

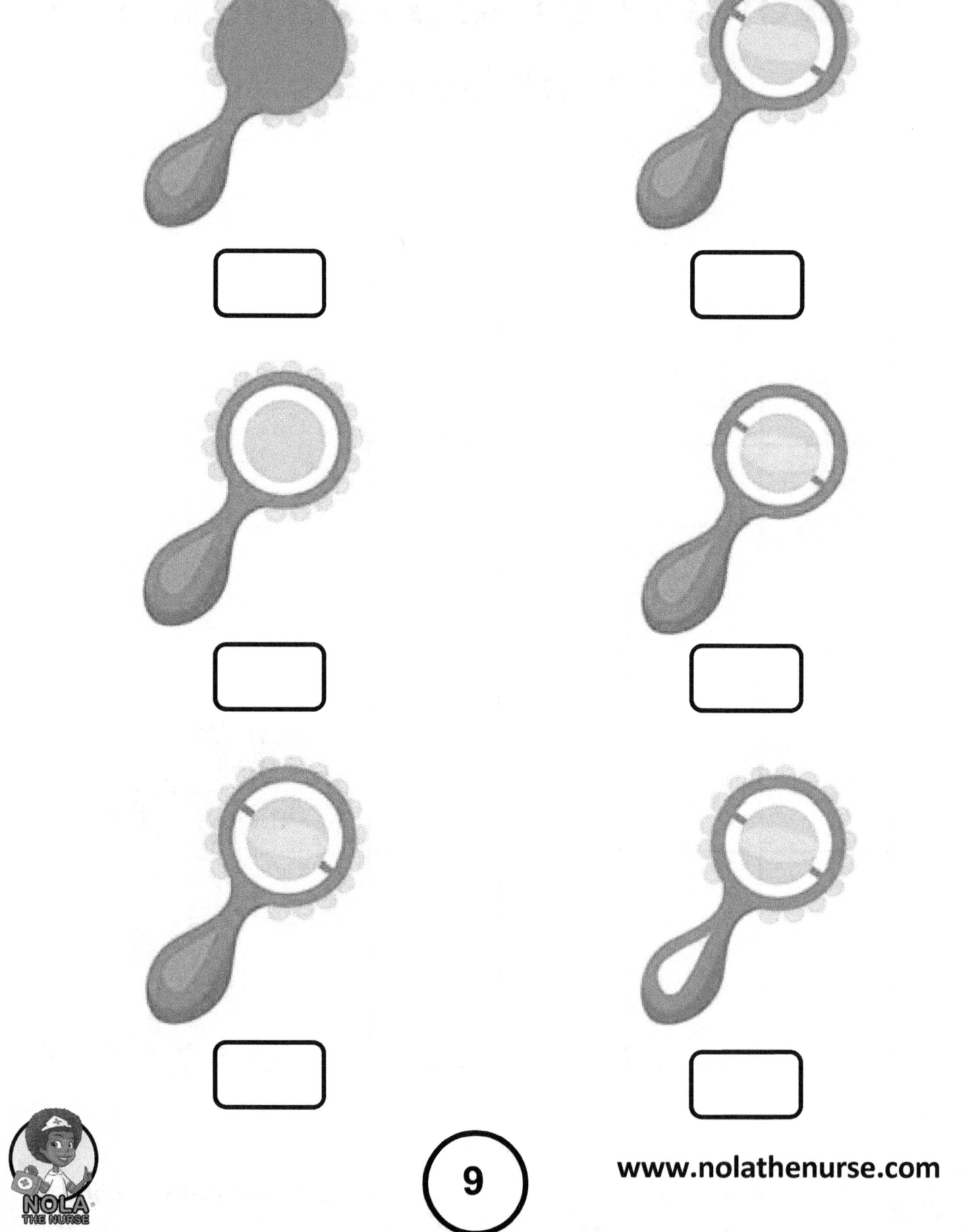

Cross [X] the odd one out.

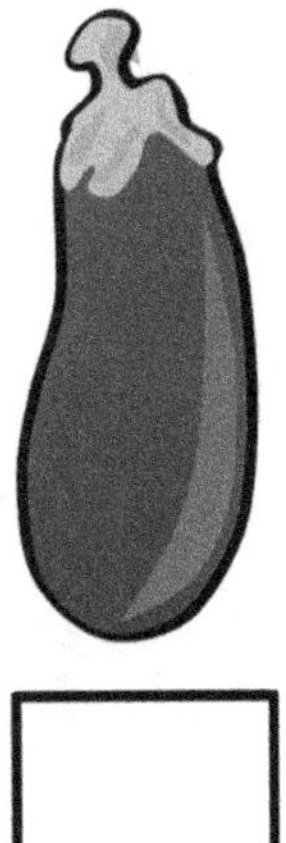

Draw the correct shapes to complete the patterns.

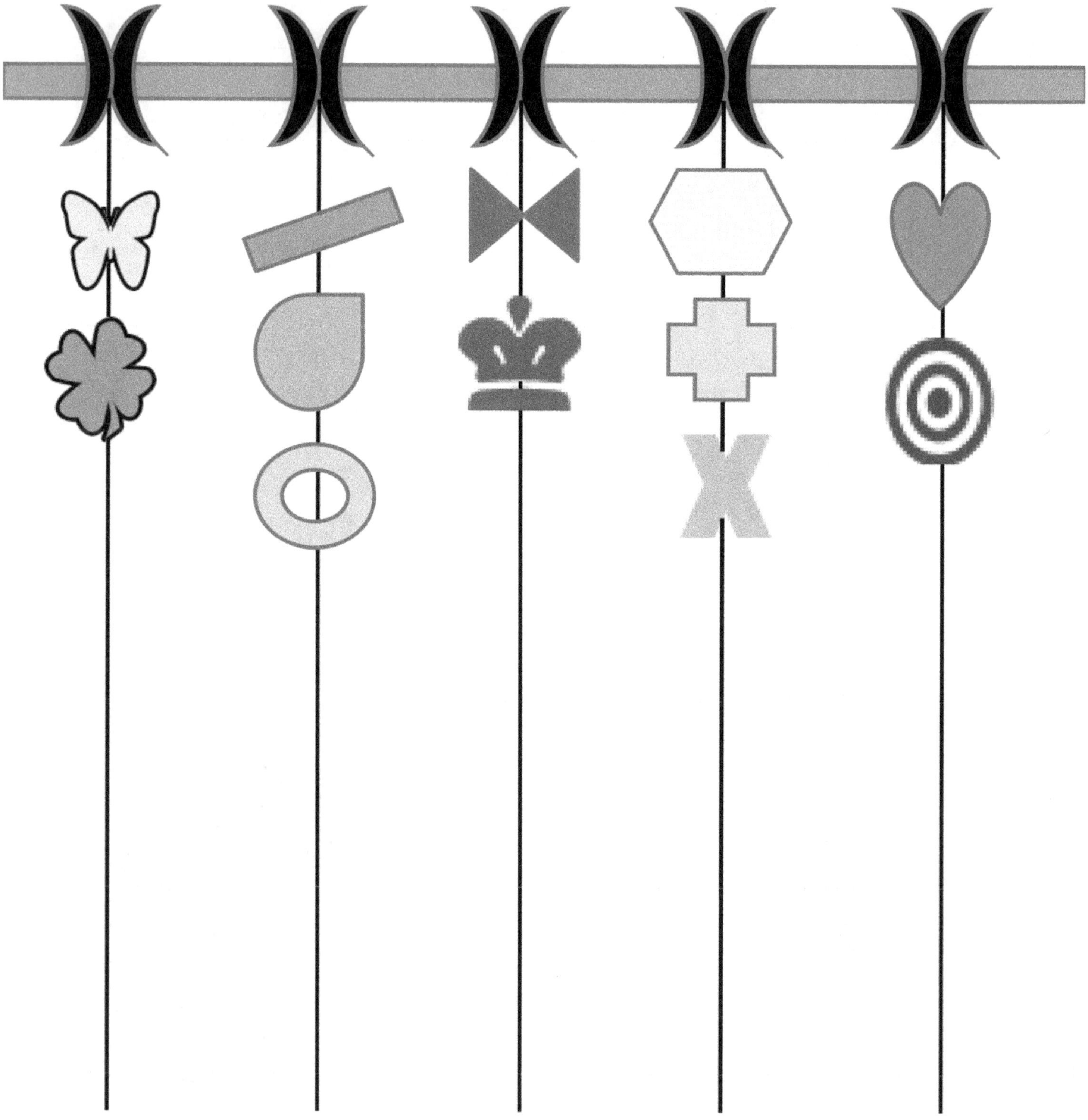

Write the first letter of each picture in the box and say aloud the name of the picture.

Draw the picture in the enlarged grid.

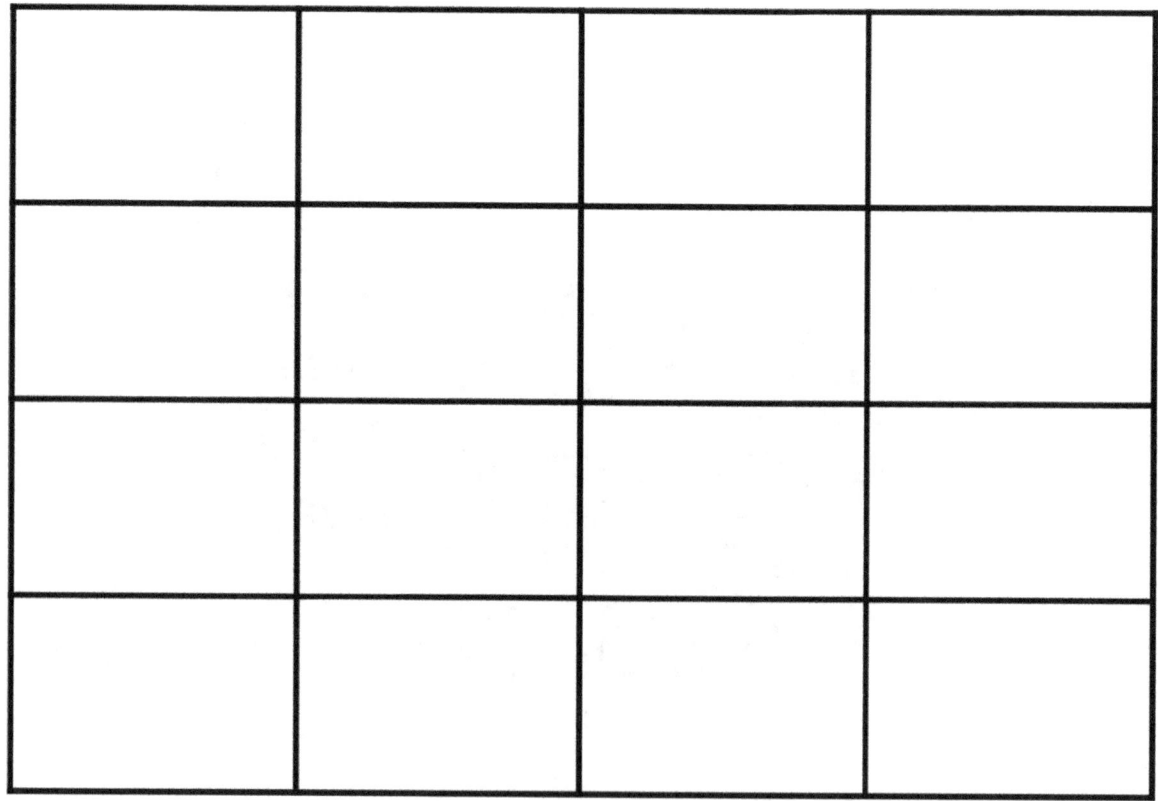

Match the picture to its correct outline.

A

B

C

D

Color the picture.

Rearrange the jumbled pieces of the given picture.

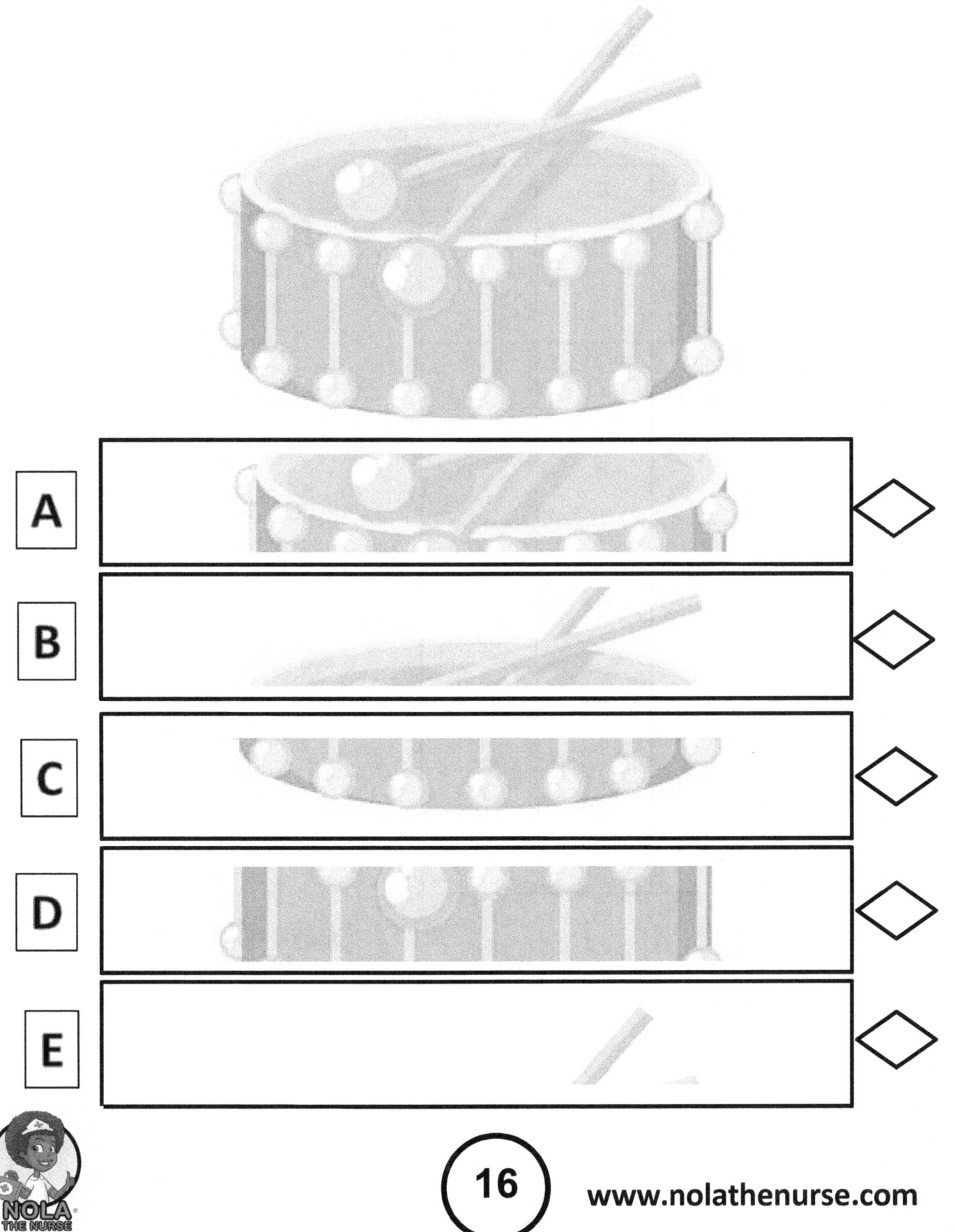

Look at the filled boxes carefully and complete the patterns in the blank boxes.

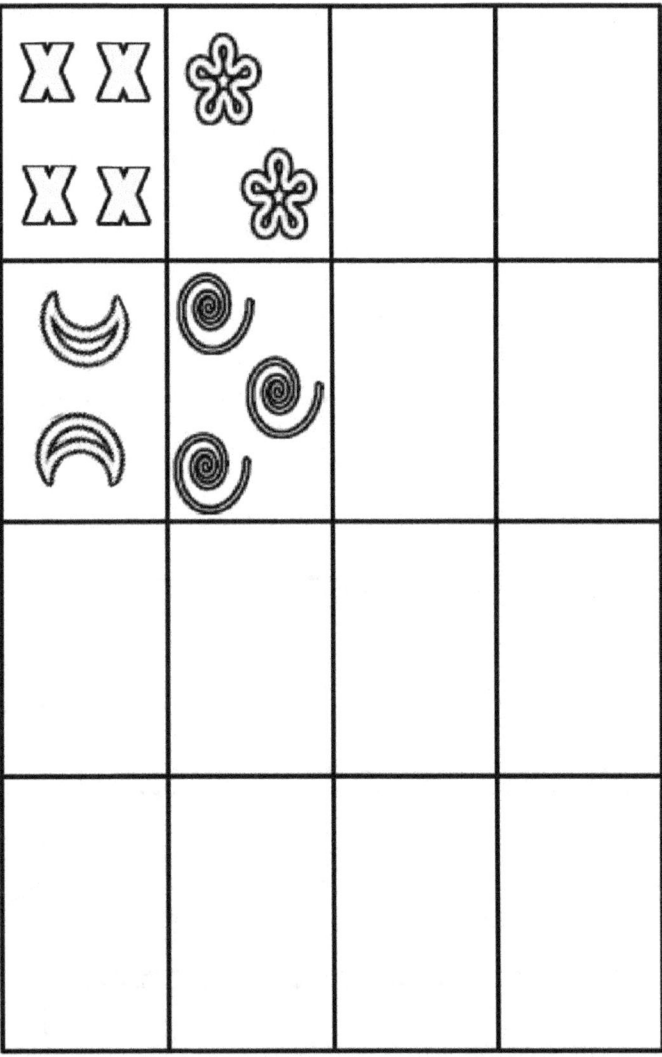

Nola The Nurse

Charo The CRNA

Make new words from the word Elephant and write in the elephant's body.

Elephant

Draw the missing picture in the given space.

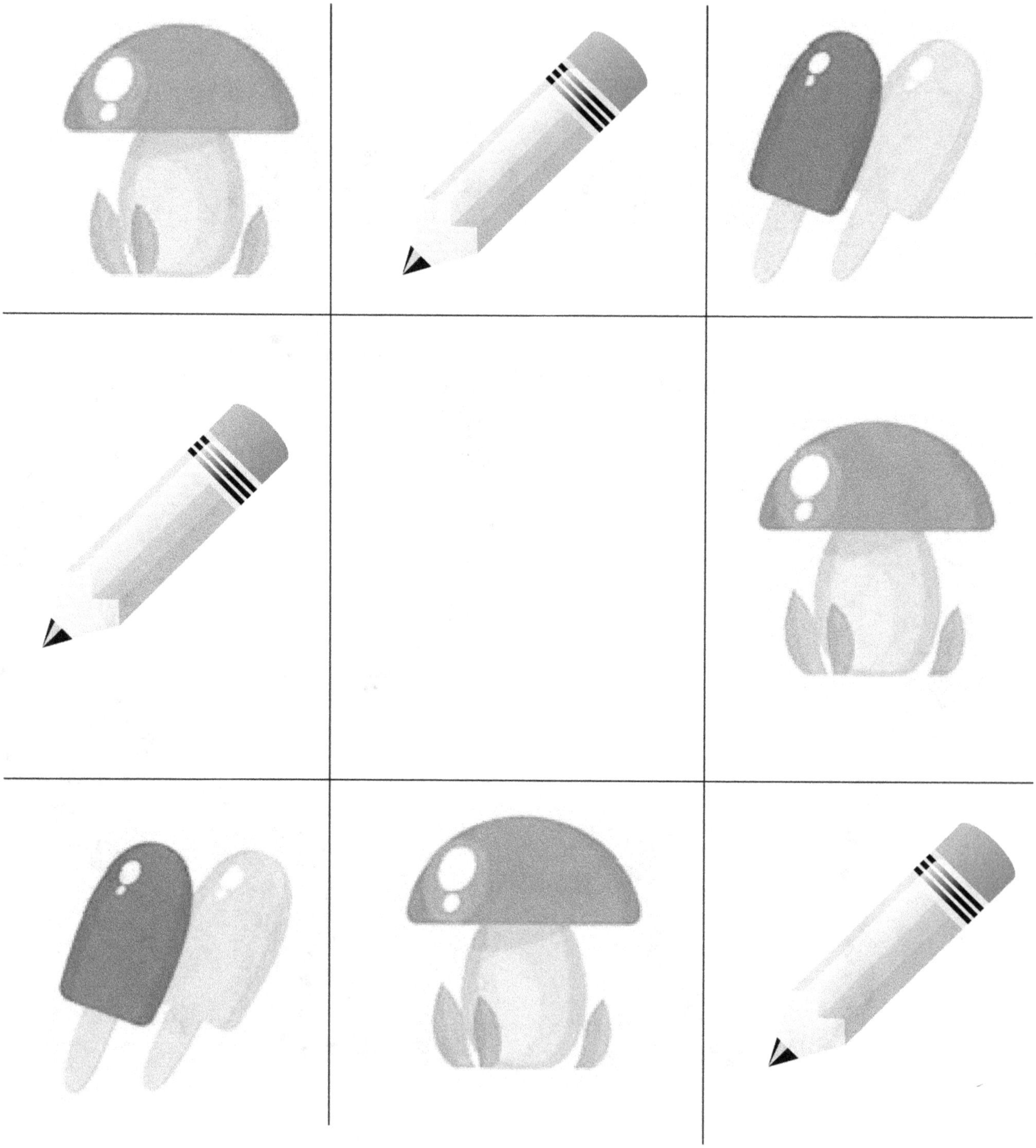

Draw the picture in the enlarged grid.

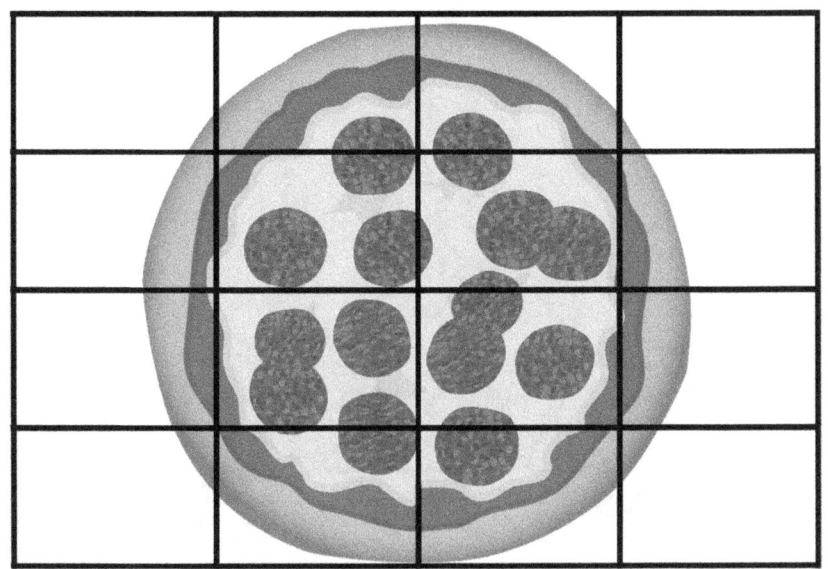

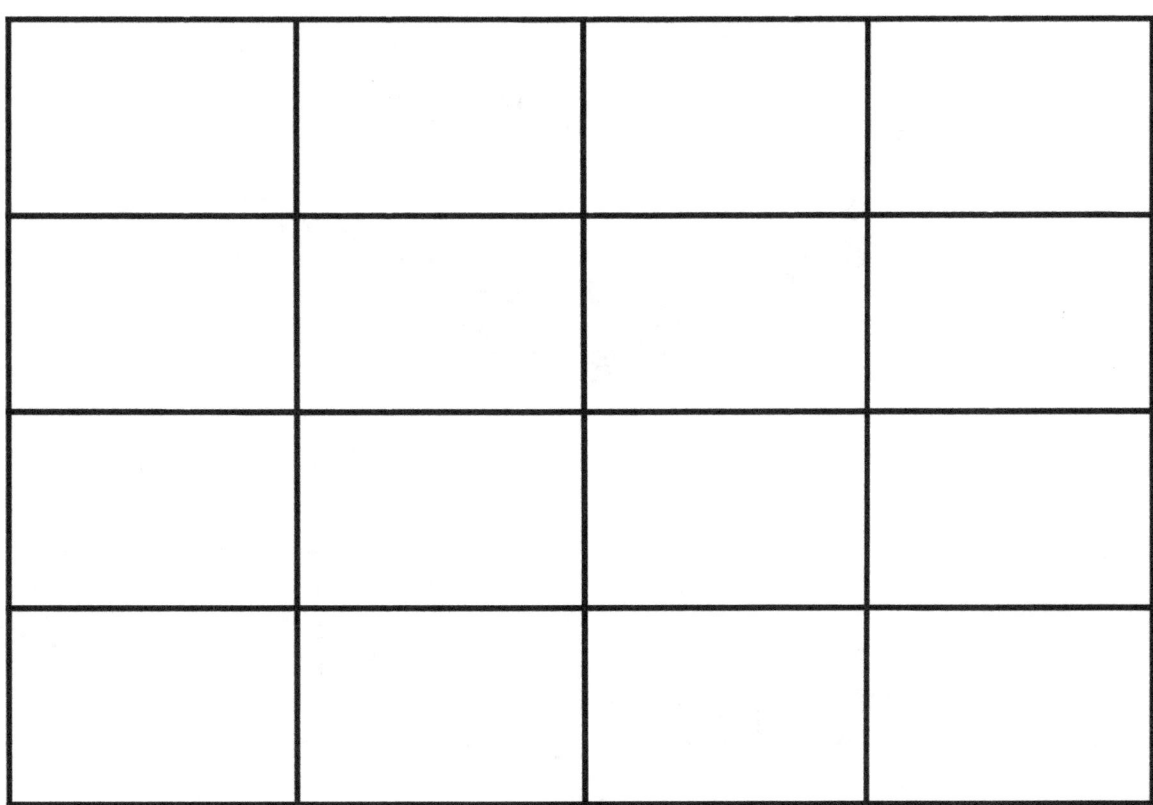

www.nolathenurse.com

Check [✓] the missing part of the picture.

○ ○ ○

Check [✓] two identical pictures.

Cross [X] the odd one out.

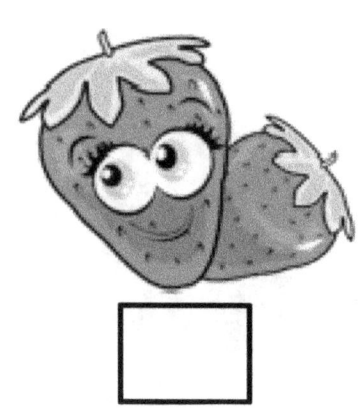
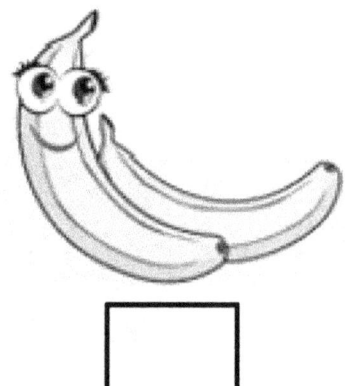

Write the first letter of each picture in the box and say aloud the name of the vegetable in the picture.

Join the dots and color the picture.

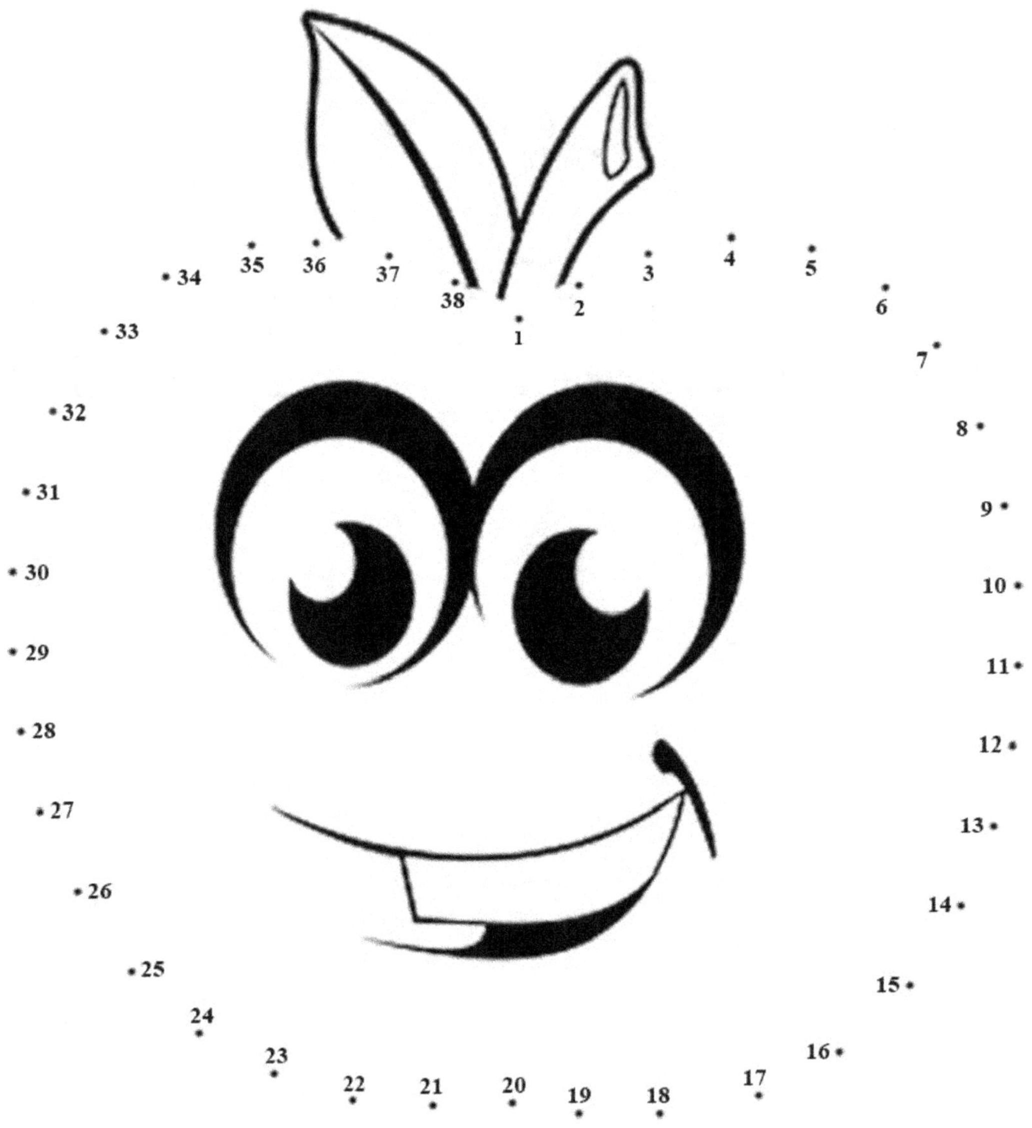

25

www.nolathenurse.com

Match the picture to its correct outline.

A

B

C

D

26

Help the girl to reach her home.

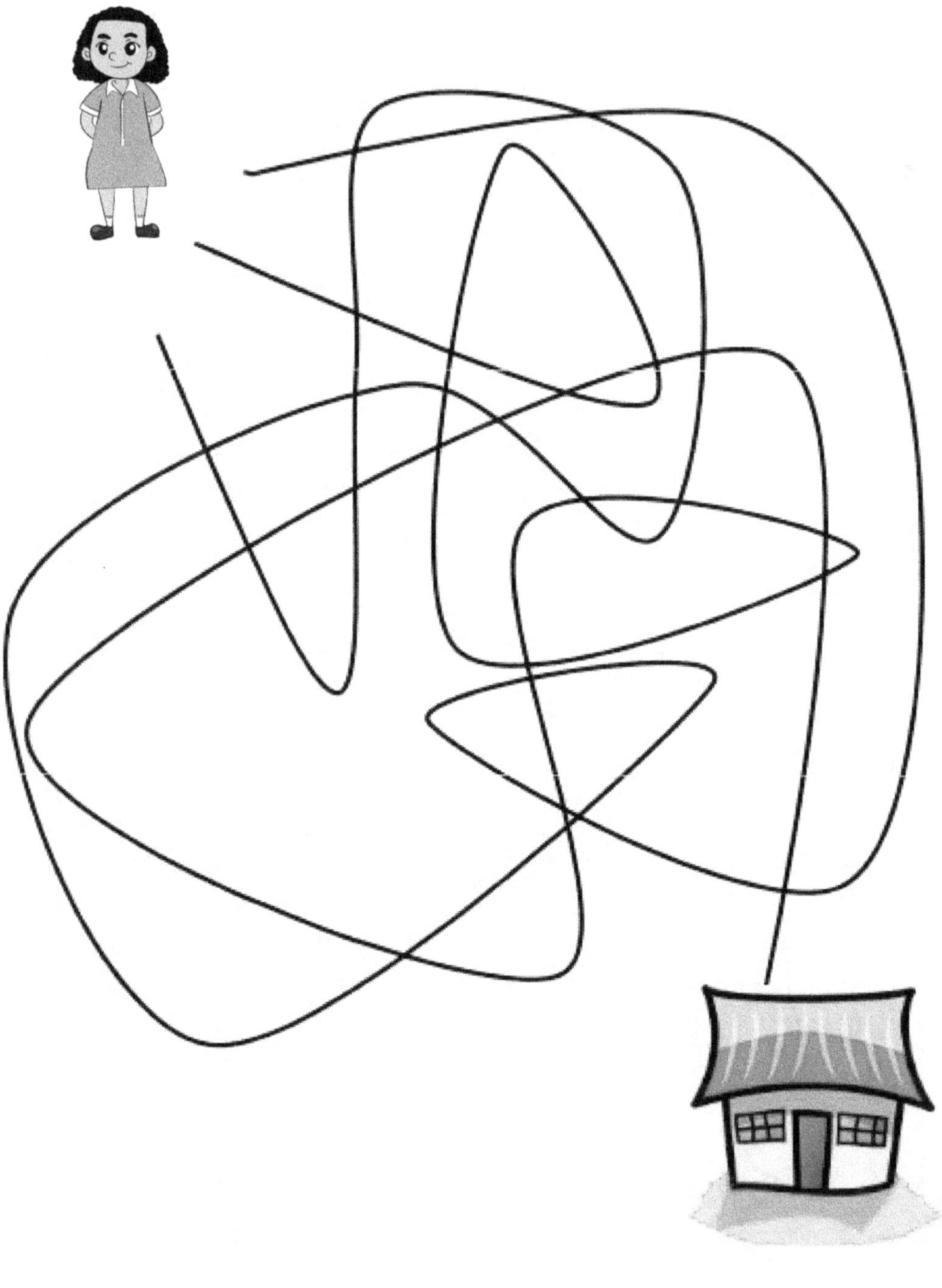

Make the picture by using the dots.

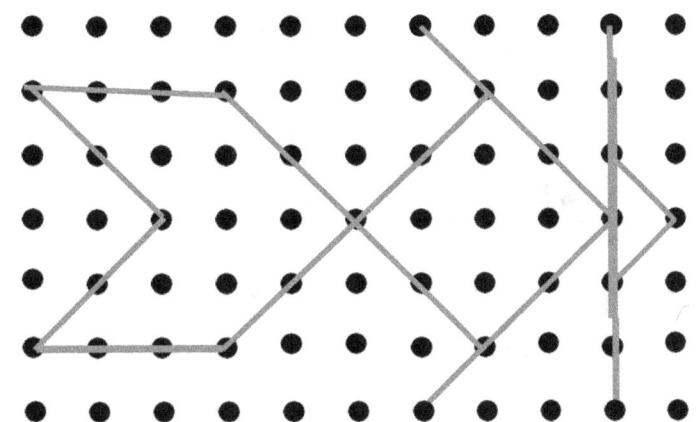

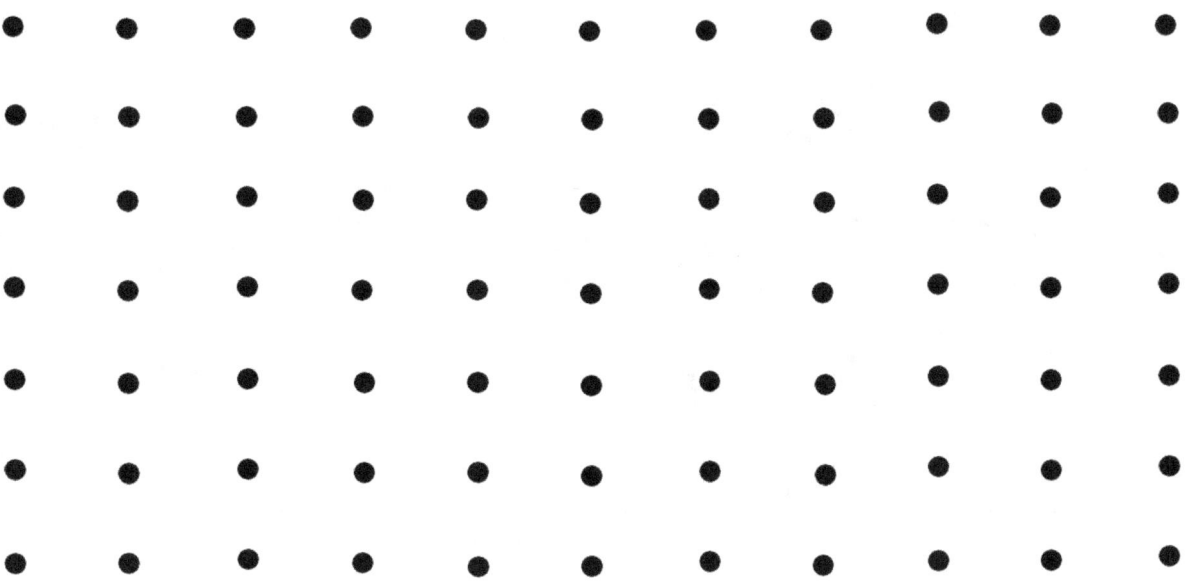

www.nolathenurse.com

Match the objects with its right names.

Gip
Pig
Igp

Otp
Top
Pot

Durm
Drum
Dmur

Blocks
Bolkcs
Bosclk

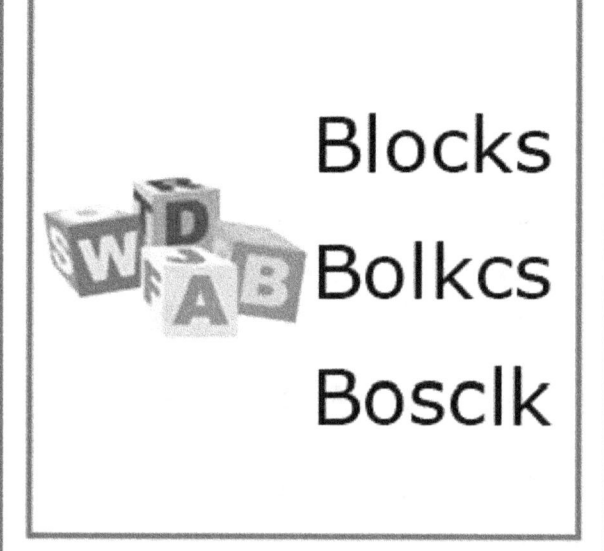

Use the object pictures to solve the puzzle.

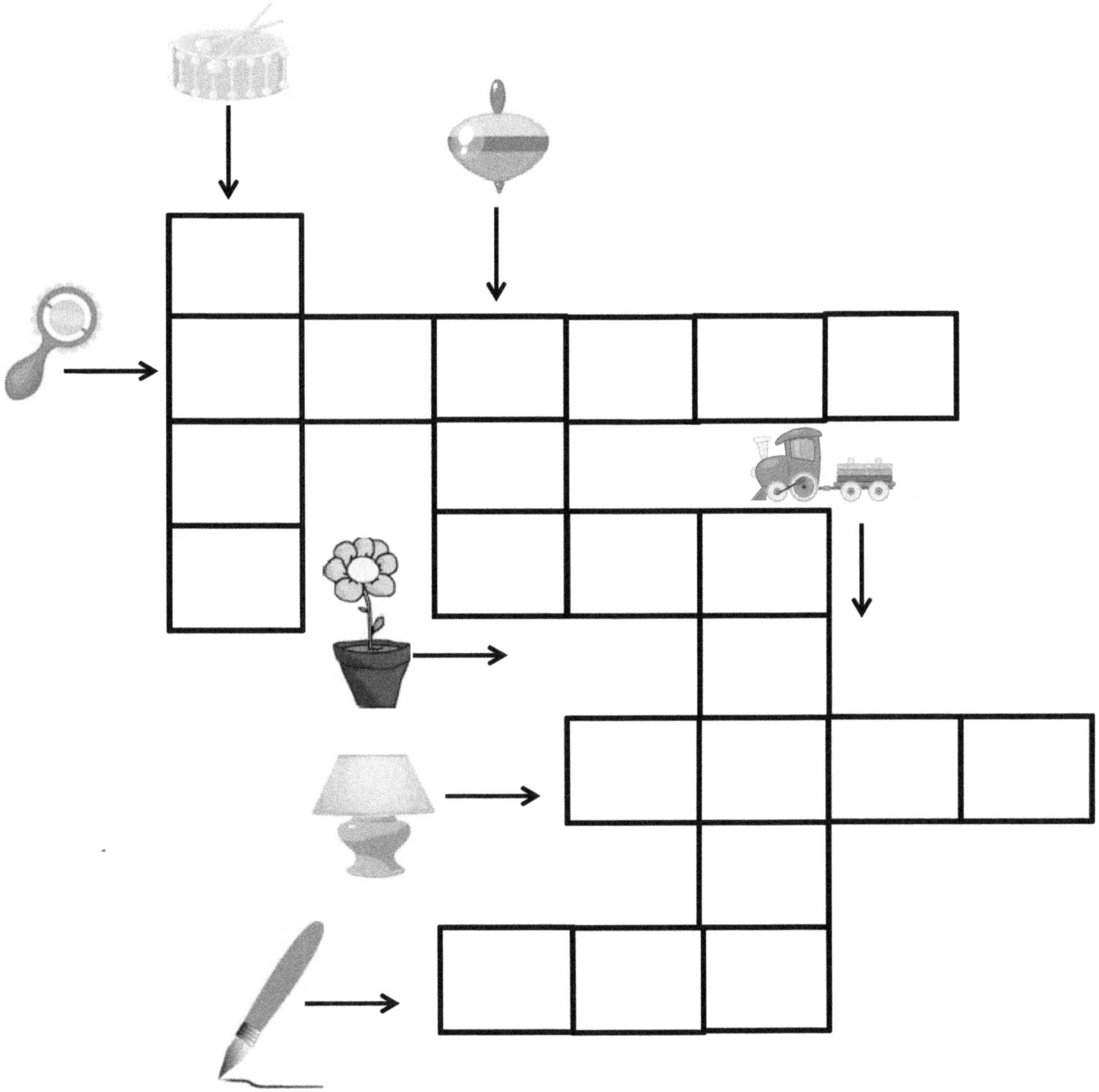

Write the correct beginning letter for the given object.

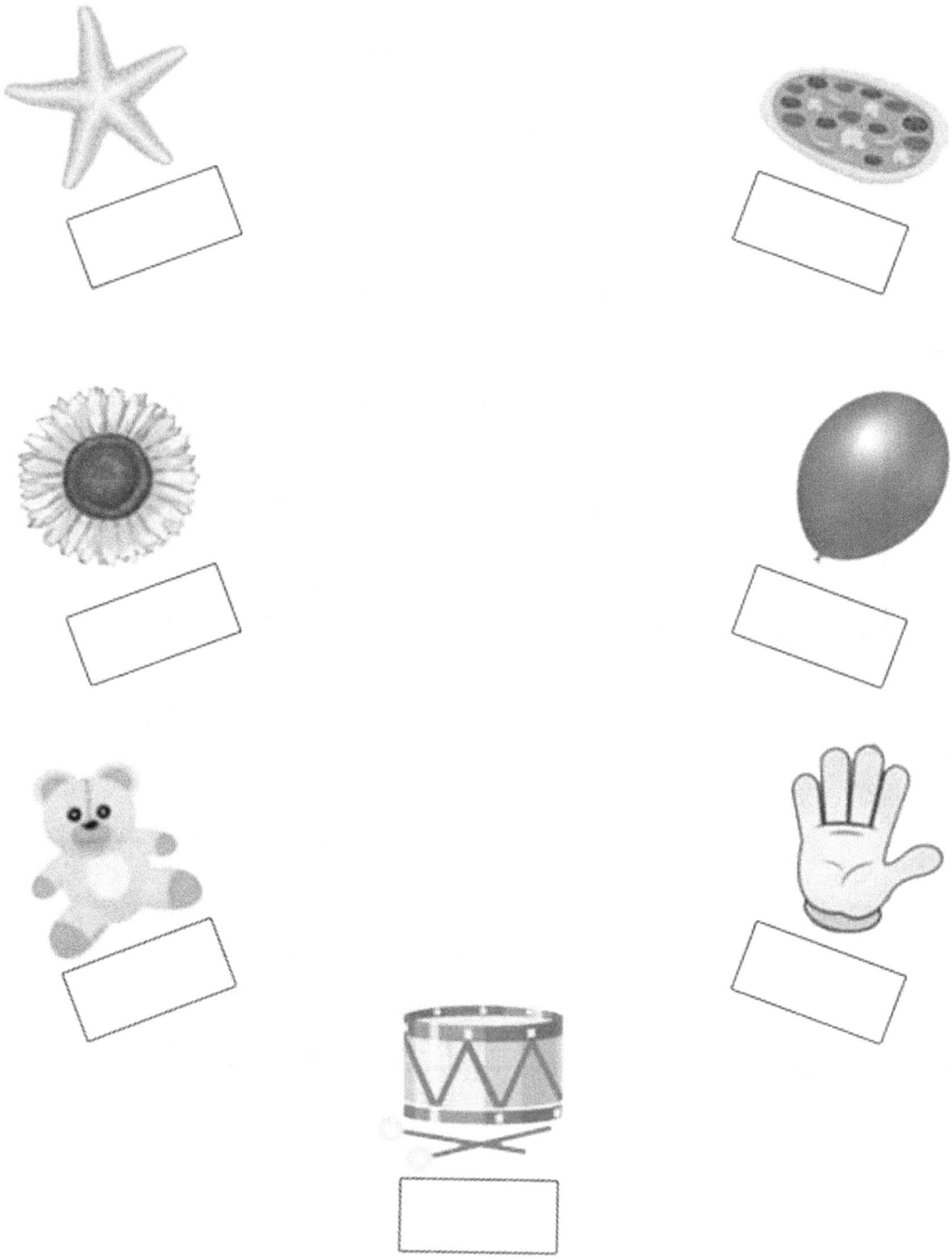

See the picture and match their names.

Leaf   Stem

Flower   Root

Plants are useful to us. Just as we have different parts in our body, plants also have some parts.

Match the objects that are the same.

Match the numbers of the given objects.

　　　　　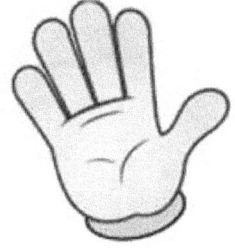

　　　　　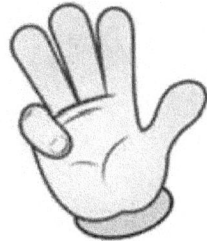

　　　　　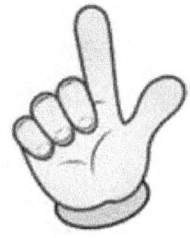

Write the number that comes after the given number.

1 ___   2 ___

5 ___   6 ___

7 ___   3 ___

9 ___   8 ___

Check the largest in each box.

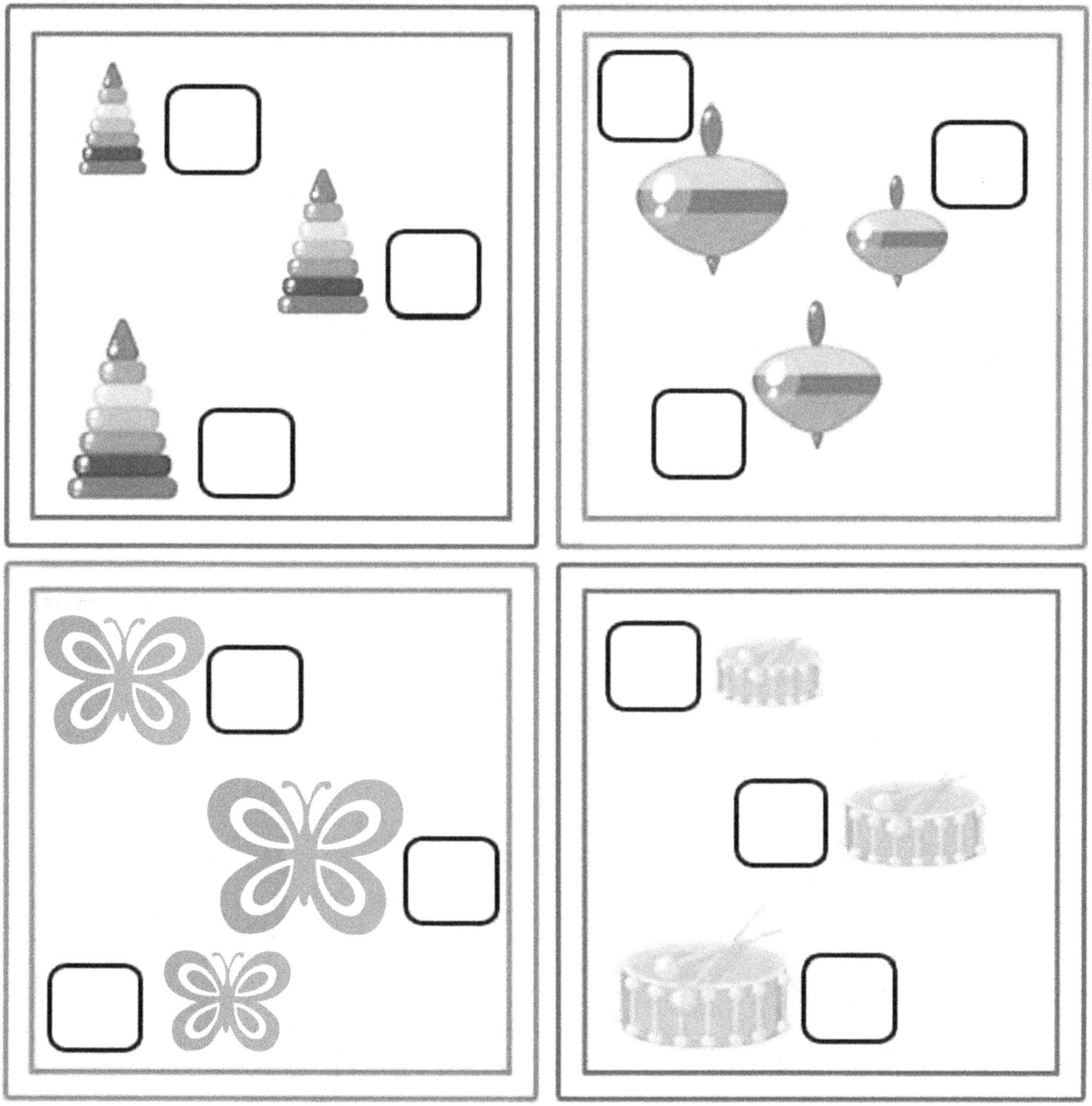

Match the same pictures.

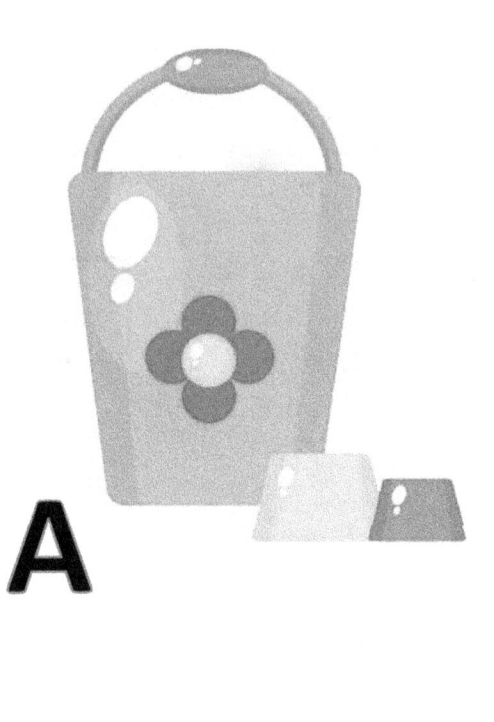

A

B

C

D

Check [✓] the missing part of the picture.

www.nolathenurse.com

Help the sheep to find food.

Find five differences between these two images.

Rearrange the jumbled pieces of the given picture.

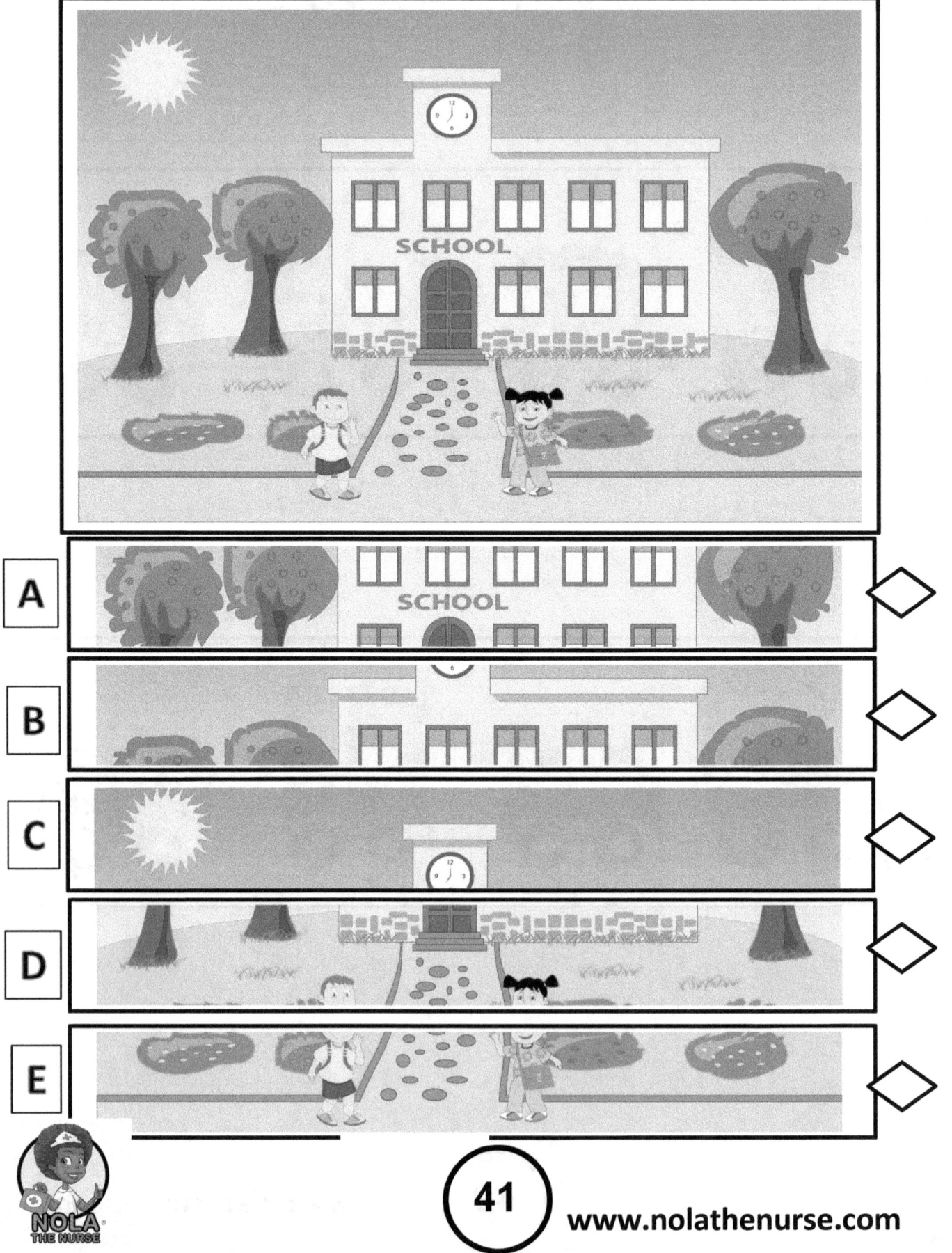

Color the Picture.

Draw the missing picture in the given space.

Spot five differences between these two pictures.

Look at the filled boxes carefully and complete the patterns in the blank boxes.

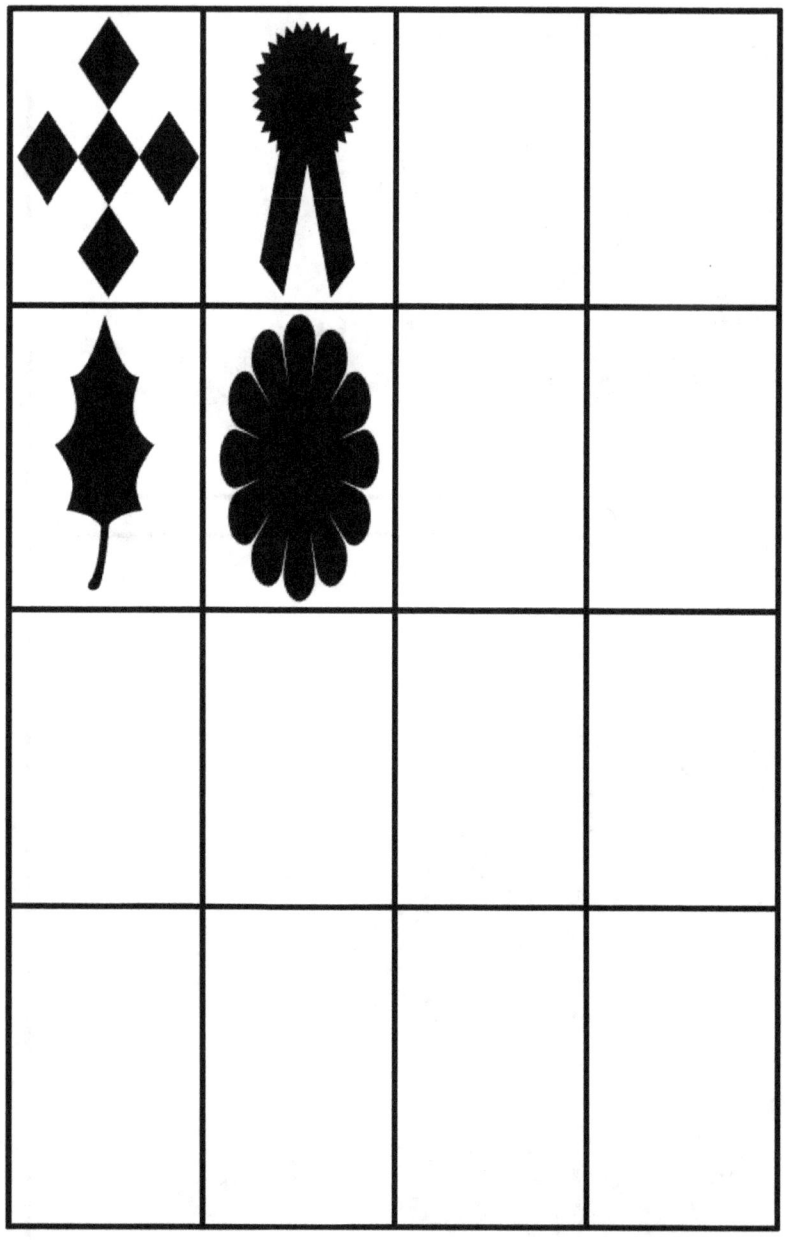

Charo The CRNA

www.nolathenurse.com

Check [✓] the two identical pictures.

www.nolathenurse.com

Cross [X] the odd one out.

Draw the correct shapes to complete the patterns.

Write the first letter of each picture in the box and say aloud

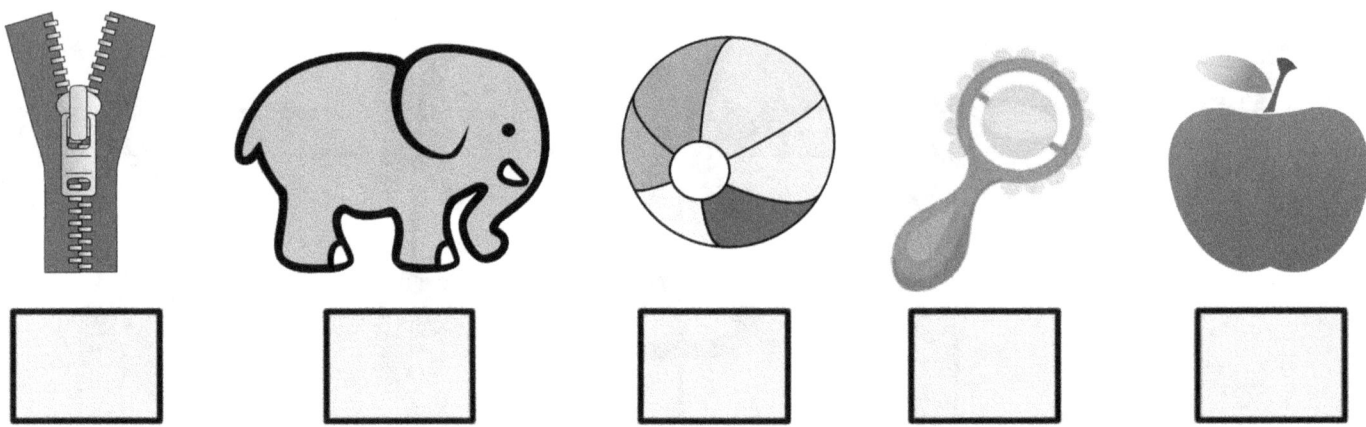

Draw the picture in the enlarged grid.

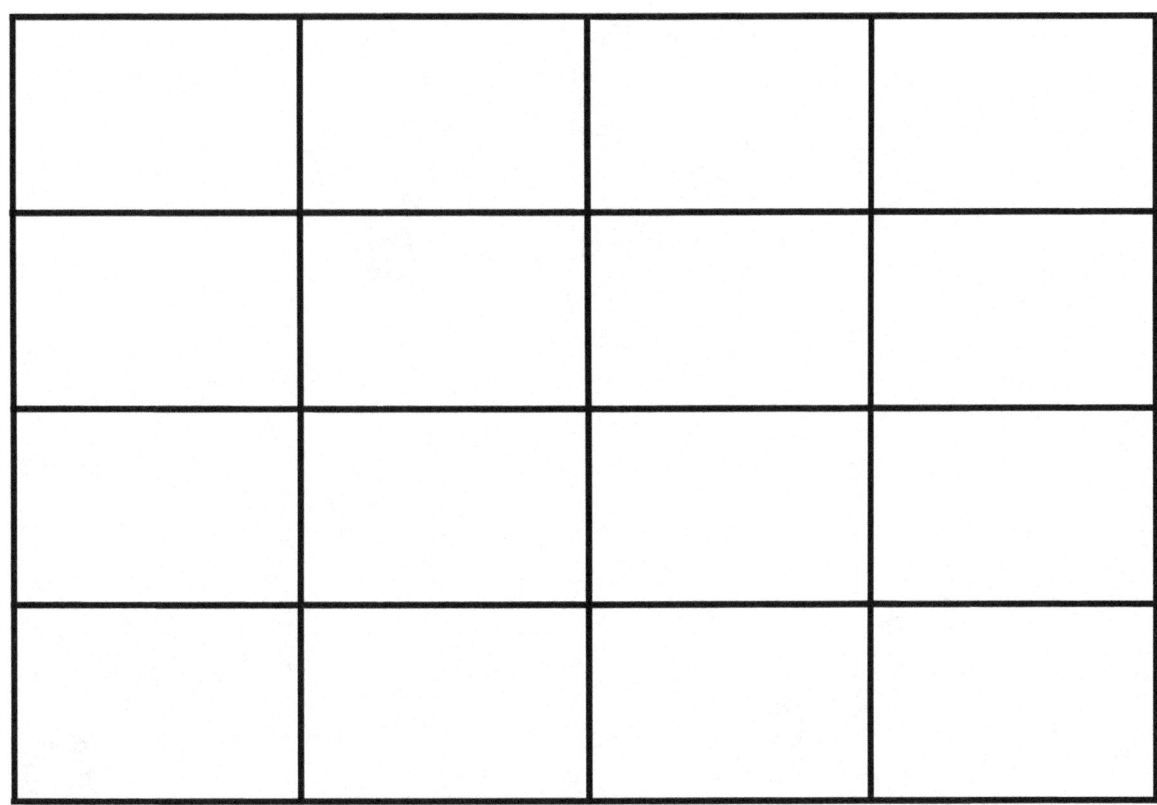

Match the picture to its correct outline.

A

B

C

D

Color the picture.

Rearrange the jumbled pieces of the given picture.

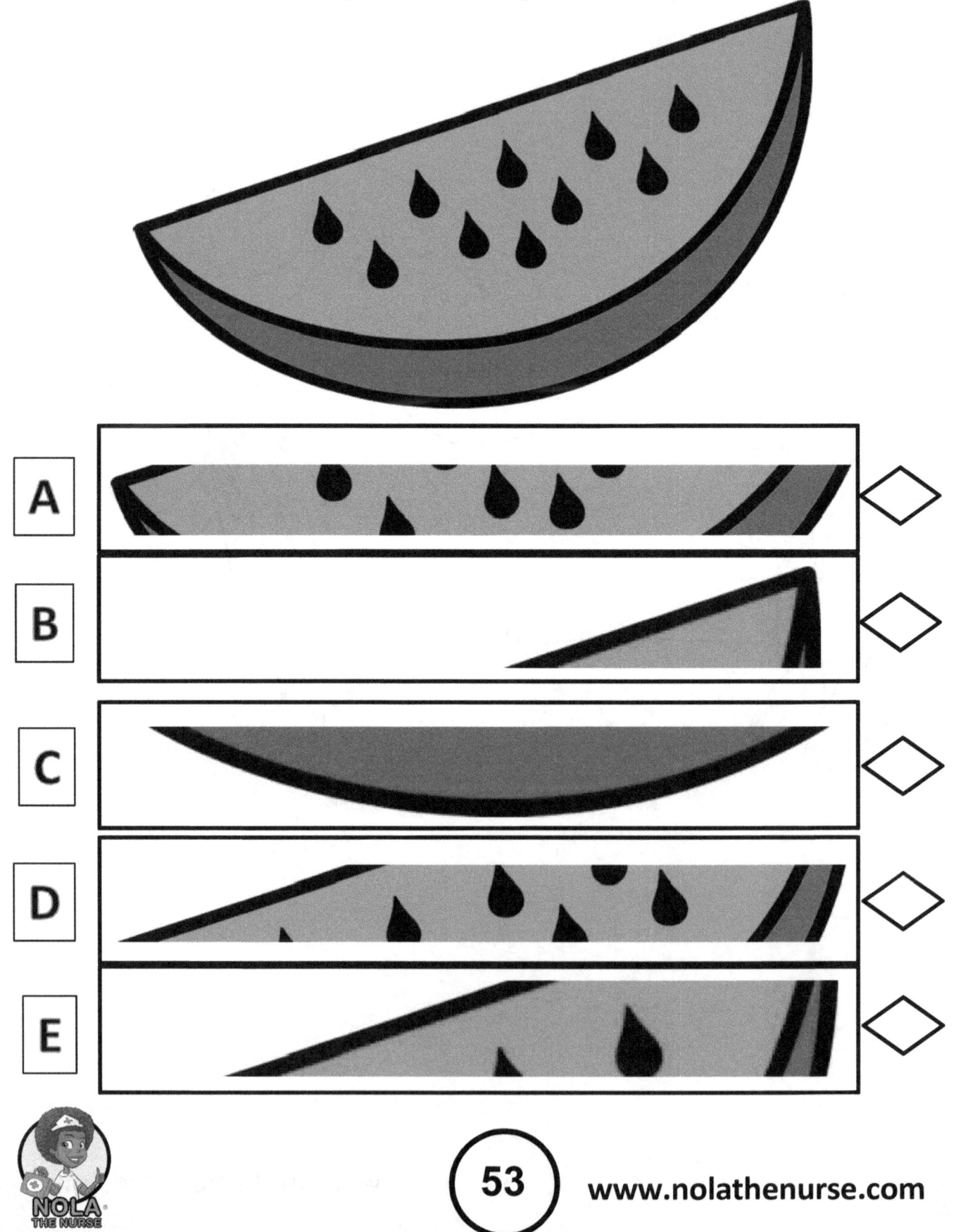

Look at the filled boxes carefully and complete the patterns in the blank boxes.

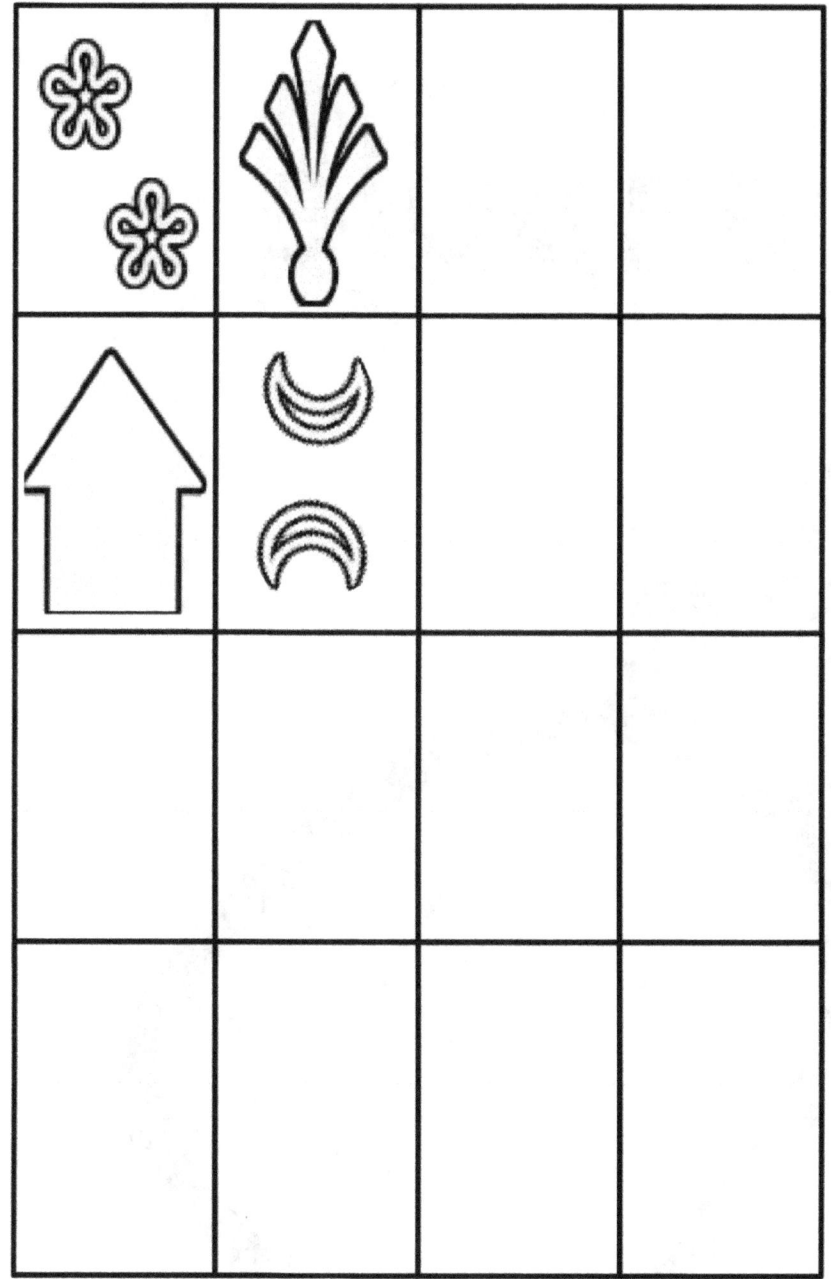

Charo The CRNA

Make new words from the word Pineapple and write on the pineapple.

Pineapple

Draw the missing picture in the given space.

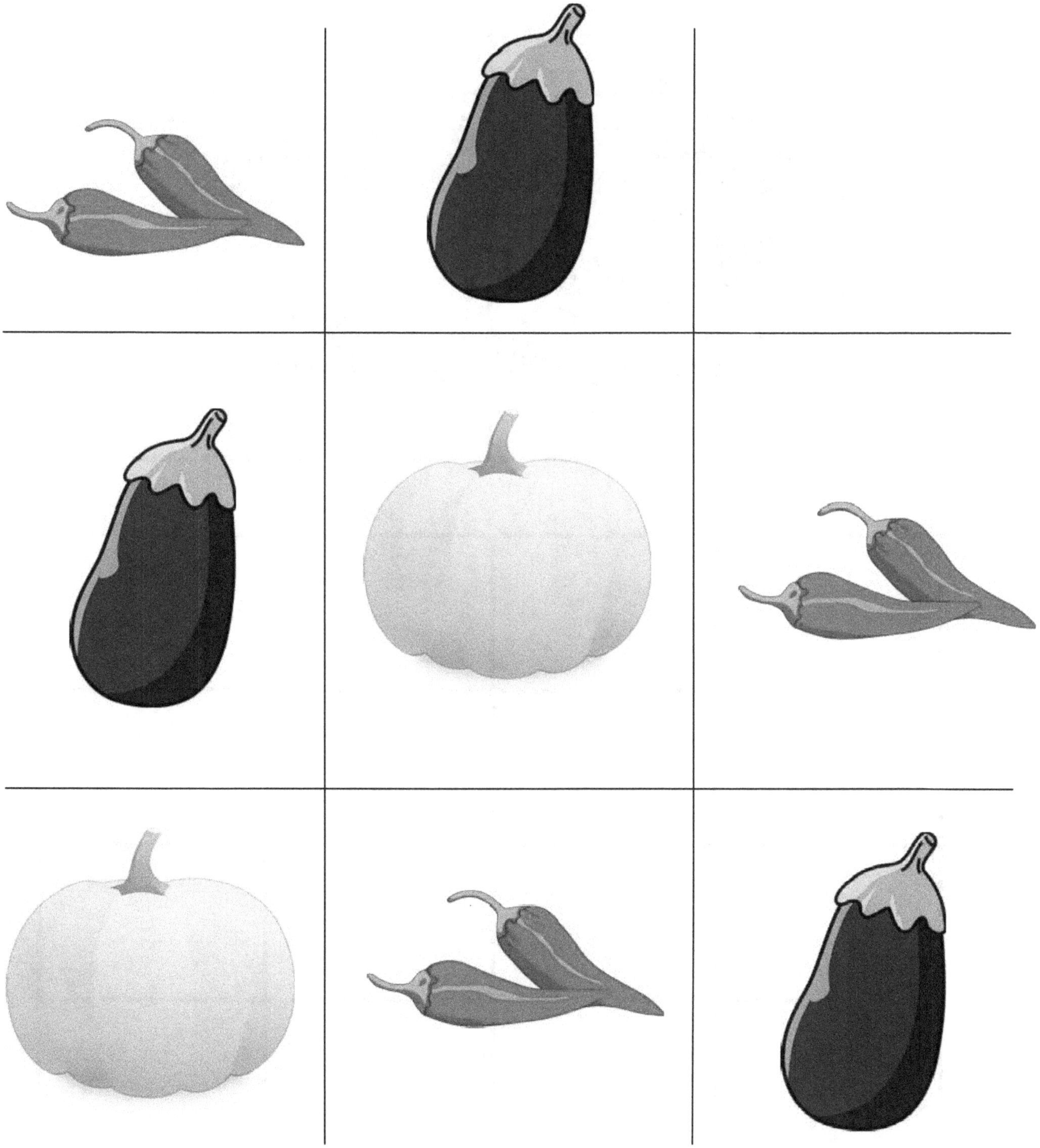

Draw the picture in the enlarged grid.

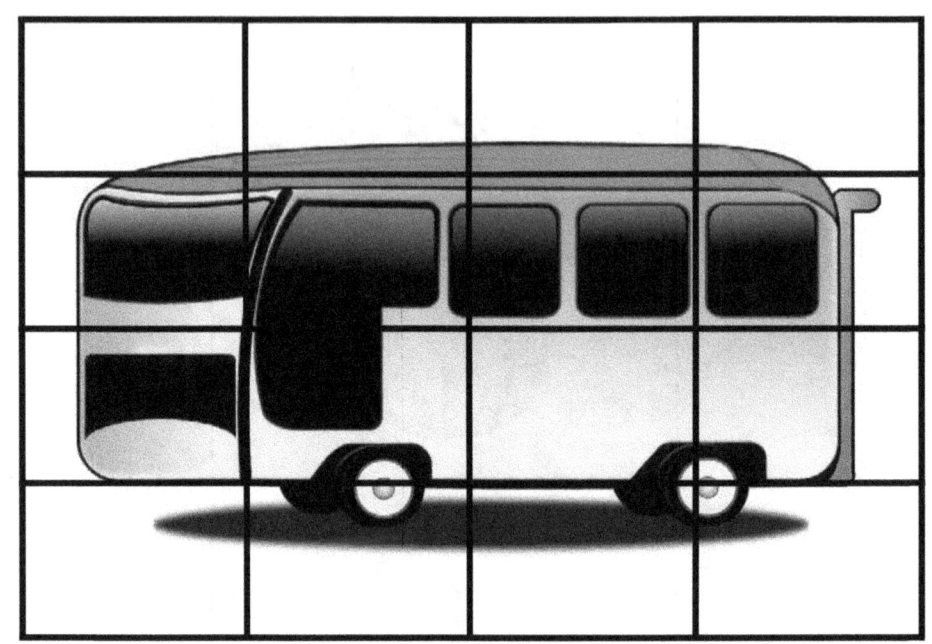

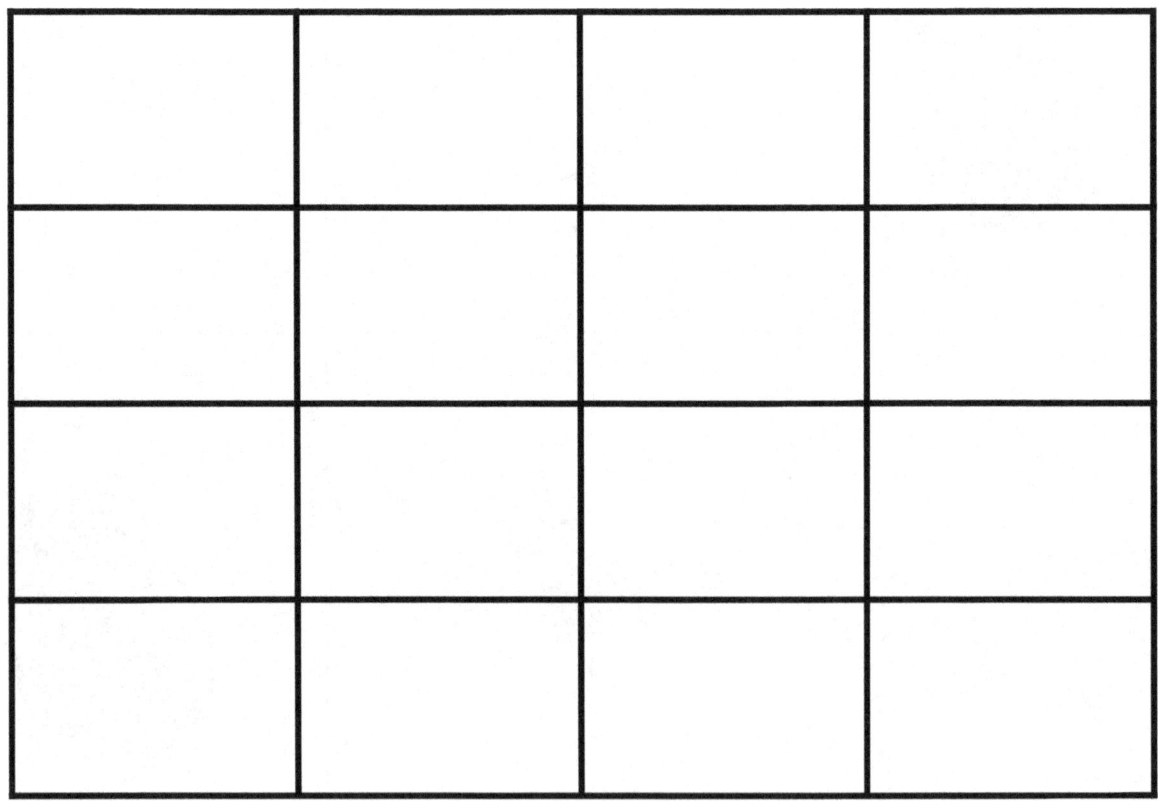

57   www.nolathenurse.com

Check [✓] the missing part of the picture.

 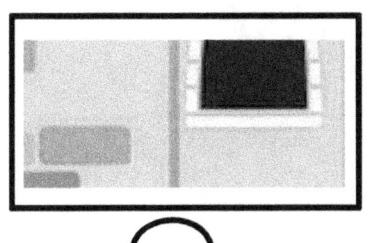 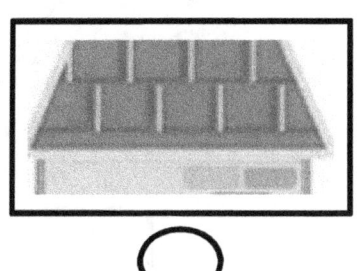

○　　　　　○　　　　　○

Check [✓] two identical pictures.

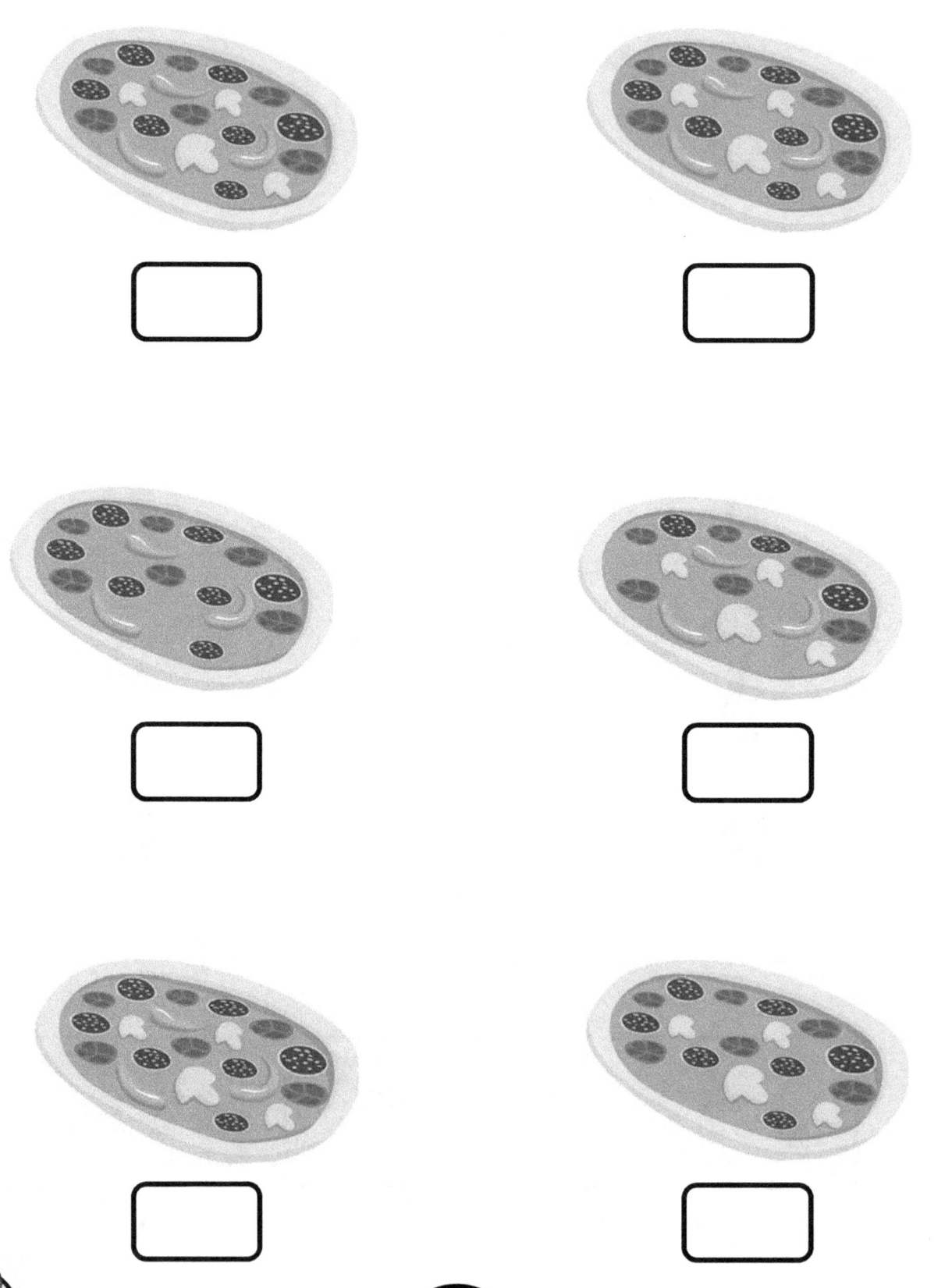

Cross [X] the odd one out.

Write the first letter of each picture in the box and say aloud the name of the fruit in the picture.

Join the dots and color the picture.

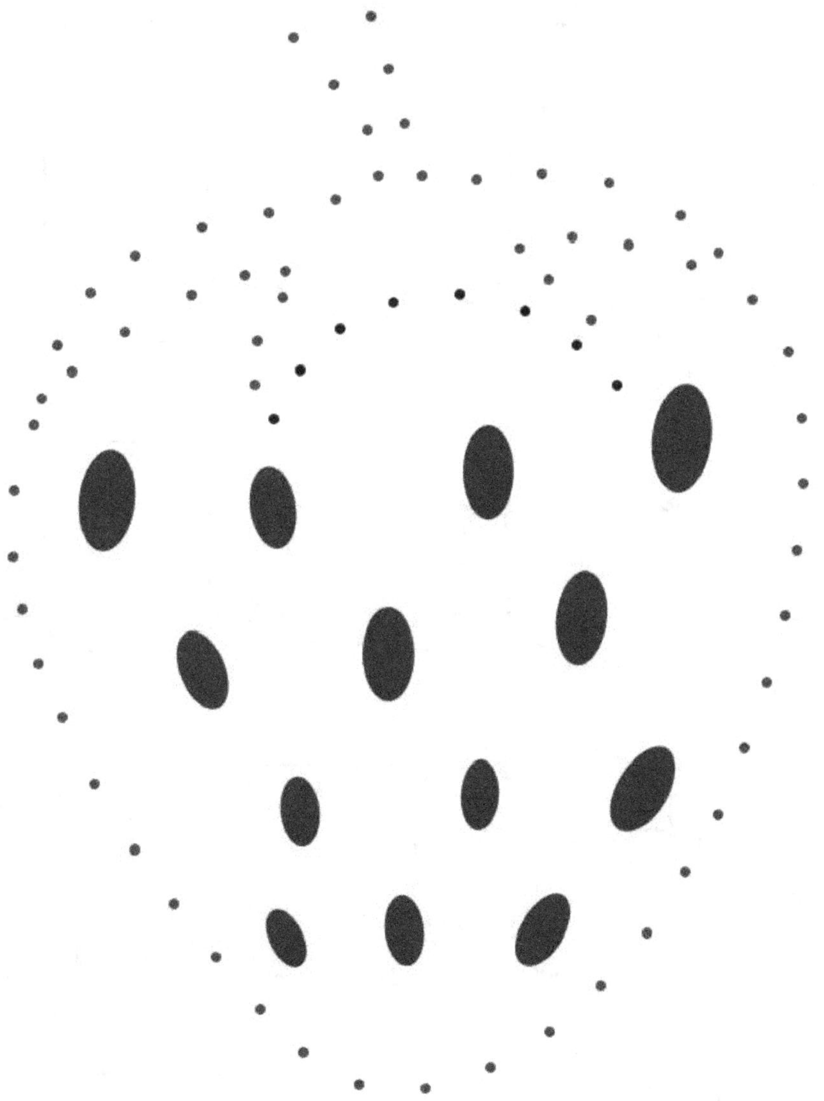

www.nolathenurse.com

Match the picture to its correct outline.

A

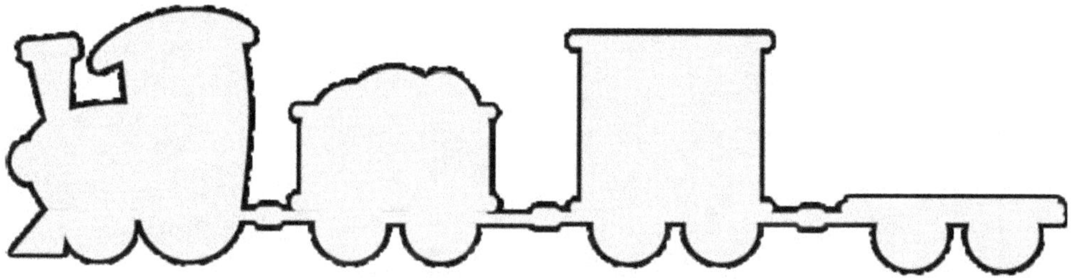

B

C

D

Help the boy to reach his home.

64 www.nolathenurse.com

Match the flowers with their names.

(daisy image)	sunflower
(tulip image)	Rose
(sunflower image)	Tulip
(lily image)	Daisy
(rose image)	lily

Use the object pictures to solve the puzzle.

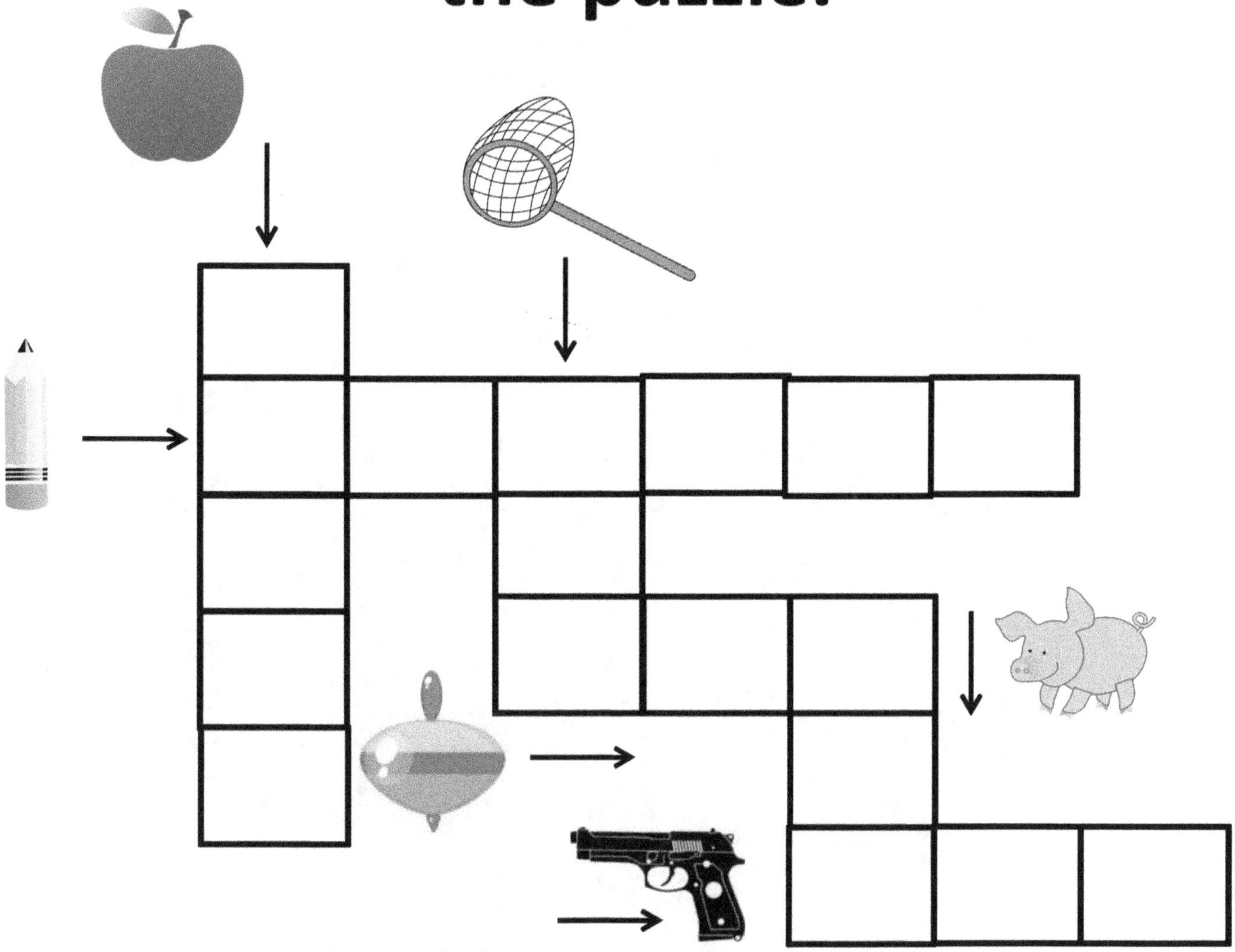

Count and write the number of A and a given in the picture.

☐ A
☐ a

Match the pictures given below with the first letter of their names.

Match the same objects.

69
www.nolathenurse.com

Match the numbers of the given objects.

   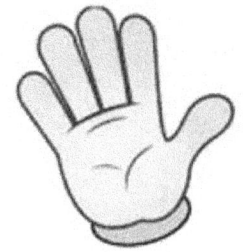

   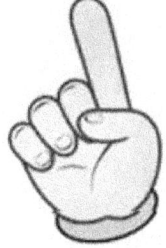

   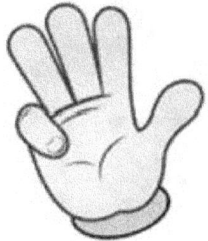

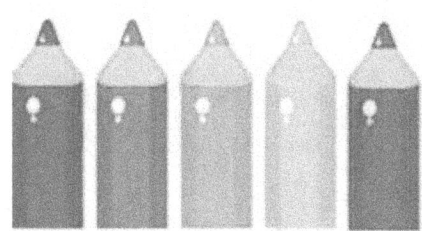   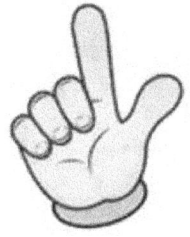

Write the number that comes before the given number.

___ 5   ___ 9

___ 2   ___ 6

___ 7   ___ 3

___ 4   ___ 8

Check [✓] the smallest in each box.

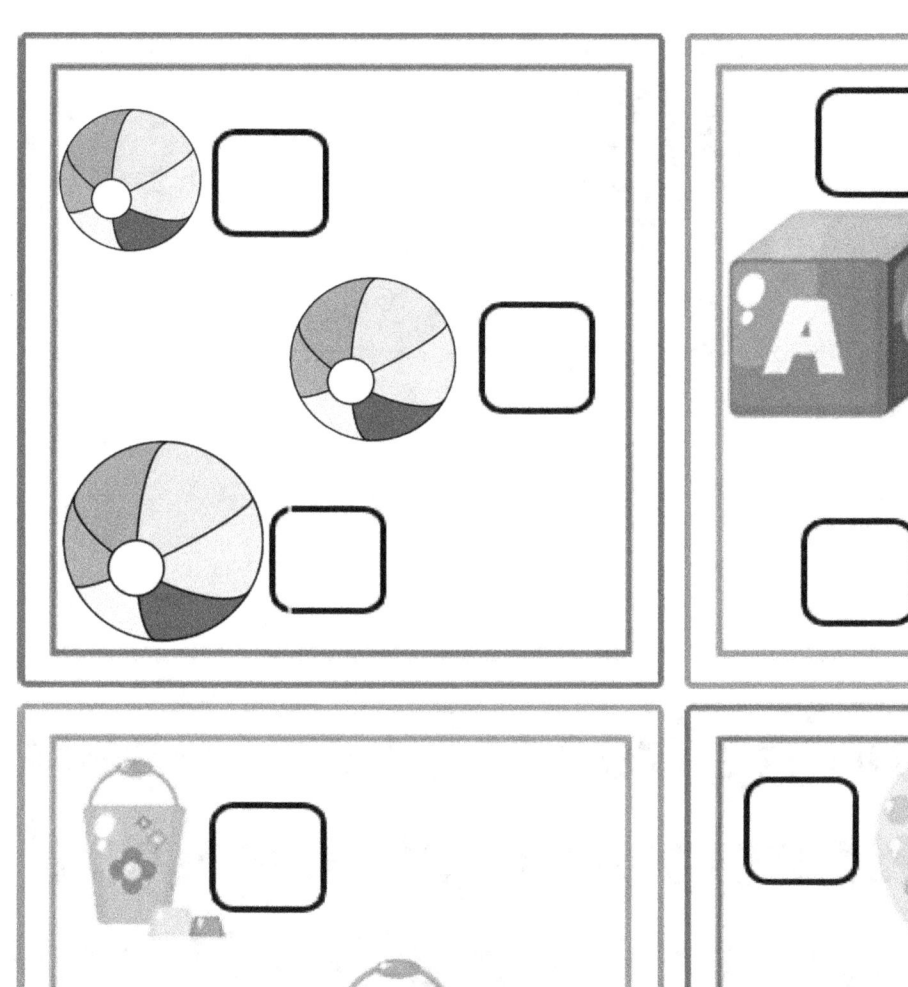

These following free color sheets are placed here to help you get to know the characters from the Nola The Nurse® children's book series. Enjoy and pick up a copy of the hottest selling children's book in America that was recently featured on The Harry Show!

Nola The Nurse

Dr. Baker Nurse Practitioner

Dr. Eden Nurse Practitioner

Bax The Nurse

Maddi the Midwife

Charo The CRNA

Gumbo

More books by Dr. Baker

Nola The Nurse® She's On The Go Series Vol 1
Nola The Nurse® & Friends Explore The Holi Fest She's On The Go Series Vol 2
Nola The Nurse® & Friends Explore The Holi Fest She's On The Go Series Vol 2 Coloring Book
Nola The Nurse® Remembers Hurricane Katrina Special Edition
Nola The Nurse® Remembers Hurricane Katrina Special Edition Coloring Book
Black Dot
Nola The Nurse® Math Activity Book for Preschoolers Vol 1

Upcoming Titles:

Nola The Nurse® Math Worksheets for Kindergarten Vol 3
Nola The Nurse® English/Sight Worksheets for Kindergarten Vol 4
Nola The Nurse® Math/English Worksheets for Preschoolers Vol 5
Nola The Nurse® Math Worksheets for First Graders Vol 6
Nola The Nurse® STEM Activity Book for 5-8 year olds Vol 7

www.NolaTheNurse.com
DrBaker@NolaTheNurse.com

About the Author

Dr. Scharmaine L. Baker, NP is a nationally recognized and award-winning nurse practitioner in New Orleans, Louisiana. She has received numerous honors and awards for her contributions to healthcare in New Orleans since she became a family nurse practitioner in 2000, including the 2013 Healthcare Hero award (New Orleans City Business magazine) and 2008 Entrepreneur of the Year award (ADVANCE for Nurse Practitioner magazine).

Dr. Baker has a doctor of nursing practice (DNP) degree from Chatham University in Pittsburgh, PA, and she is a fellow of the American Association of Nurse Practitioners (AANP). She was inspired to make house calls while caring for her grandmother, who was ill and needed an in-home doctor.

After Hurricane Katrina, Dr. Baker was instrumental in caring for the sick and disabled in New Orleans, where hospitals had closed and doctors had evacuated but never returned. Her patient load went from 100 to 500 in only three months. Thanks to her passion and unwavering dedication to caring for homebound patients in her home town, Dr. Baker's story was featured on the CBS Evening News with Katie Couric.

Today, Dr. Baker maintains a busy private practice in New Orleans by making house calls to the elderly and disabled who would otherwise not receive healthcare.

When this award-winning and nationally known nurse practitioner is not on the road delivering keynote speeches and attending various other media events, she loves reading to her children, Skylar Rose and Wyatt Shane.

www.DrBakerNP.com
www.NolaTheNurse.com
https://shop.nolathenurse.com

www.ingramcontent.com/pod-product-compliance
Lightning Source LLC
Chambersburg PA
CBHW081339080526
44588CB00017B/2675